Thinking in Images:
The Path to Being

Thinking in Images: The Path to Being

A journey from Inside our Heads Out into Life into the Present Moment

Alberto Botero

Lulu Press, Inc. 3101 Hillsborough Street, Raleigh, NC 27607
For information about special discounts available for bulk purchases, sales promotions, fund-raisings and educational needs, contact ThinkingInImages.org at thinkinginimags@gmail.com or call 1-800-915-5217

Visit the author's website at www.thinkinginimages.org

First edition

Published in 2016 by Lulu Press, Inc.

ISBN #: 978-1-365-46889-6

This book is dedicated to my dad. Dad, you taught me that anything is possible, that my beliefs and the belief of others can share the same space without conflict bond by mutual respect. You taught me that learning never ends and that the human mind is a thing of marvel.

Leonel la vida
empieza cuando
Tu lo decides
Toda la suerte del
mundo en lo que
hagas   alberto
9/9/17

Table of Contents

Acknowledgments

I was fortunate to have a couple of teachers that inspired me to explore when I was just starting high school, my philosophy teacher and my history teacher, two men that loved what they do and gave selflessly.

My commercial law teacher at the University for challenging all we believe, for going beyond his subject to make us thinkers.

Joe Palmer, your friendship and your excitement about the theory, and especially your contribution in structuring the work and editing made these last steps a lot easier.

My kids Juan Alejandro, Emerald and Camilla, my grandkids, Emilia and Luciano, you are a source of inspiration. I hope that my work may contribute even in the tiniest way to make this a better world for you to enjoy.

Rosie my wife you have been a supporter and believer from day one. Thank you for your patience.

Dr. Jorge Victoria without your selfless support and your generosity, without your knowledge and your offer to take me under your wing, this book would not have been possible.

You took me in as a patient three times a week when I could afford only a few dollars per session. Every time I have a client that is scrapping to pay a few dollars, I remember the lessons I learned by watching the delight you took on getting those few dollars I could afford in your hand. It was the exchange of efforts that you were happy about, you gave your all to me, your patient, your student.

Introduction

We are unique in the sense that we have the ability to turn our attention onto ourselves; to question ourselves, not in a judgmental way but instead with curiosity. We are the only species that can reflect on its own actions. We question our own thoughts and actions. This is a true gift.

By doing this, we can escape the prison of our memories and our mind, and experience a new view of the world.

We all have the ability to unwrap a great gift, the present. The biggest present of all is the present moment. The only place where we exist at least is what we know now.

We are bound, tied down by our memories, our mind whispering in our ear all sorts of things. One of the things the mind tells us is that, it is dangerous out there. We decide not to take risks unless there is a guarantee of no pain and no fear. We learn to discredit what we want and make our life smaller and smaller; we want less and less for the sake of safety. Like little kids will say when they are not chosen for a game of ball, "After all, I didn't want to play anyway."

In the present moment, we see people as they are, not as they were. In the present moment, I can see me as I am, not as I once was. In the present moment, I am resourceful because I can use what I have learned from my previous tries.

Judgments tend to keep me from trying again. Judgments are the result of our inability to embrace our results. Results are neither good nor bad. Often I categorize results as bad if they don't give me what I expect.

Often enough, we bury ourselves in layers and layers of judgments so thick that we are unable to experience any other reality except the grim, overwhelming feeling of despair, as if every task is bigger than we are.

The present is where you happen. You become as you are happening. We are here on this journey to realize that the thoughts that are occurring in our heads are like a virtual reality game. The game is so advanced and what we smell and feel emotionally and physically is so real that we think it is reality.

Granted, it is extremely difficult not to think it's reality; after all, it is happening in your head.

To reclaim reality, we get to take off the helmet and goggles that are projecting this virtual world inside our heads. It is simple, yet, not easy.

To accomplish this, we get to create a different relationship with our brain. We get to realize that not every thought the brain produces needs to be attended to.

You will realize that your brain acts like a nervous, pessimistic, insecure, anxiety-ridden friend that often pokes you in the stomach or presses your chest with emotions of fear, constantly whispering her thoughts into your ear and insisting that you have to believe everything she says without questioning and take her directions.

Don't concern yourself trying to find an answer to your current situation, you already left that station on the journey of your life. We are looking at those stations only to learn from them, so you mistakenly won't visit them again. We want you to be able to chart your next trip to the destination you want. As you move through this journey, you will discover to your surprise that you are wiser, thoughtful and more resourceful than you thought you were and this will change your life and the lives around you.

That would be the answer you have been looking for, to experience every moment anew.

ONE: Your Intellectual understanding of who you think you are would not support you in living the life you want

This book is not linear, although you may want it to be. It doesn't connect things as you are used to. It may upset you. It will stir things up, challenging what you know. It repeats itself because that is what we do, that is how we learn.

"How can a three-pound mass of jelly that you can hold in your palm imagine angels, contemplate the meaning of infinity, and even question its own place in the cosmos? Especially awe-inspiring is the fact that any single brain, including yours, is made up of atoms that were forged in the hearts of countless, far-flung stars billions of years ago. These particles drifted for eons and light-years until gravity and change brought them together here, now. These atoms now form a conglomerate- your brain- that can not only ponder the very stars that gave it birth but can also think about its own ability to think and wonder about its own ability to wonder.

With the arrival of humans, it has been said, the universe has suddenly become conscious of itself. This, truly, is the greatest mystery of all."

THE TELL-TALE BRAIN: A NEUROSCIENTIST'S QUEST FOR WHAT MAKES US HUMAN BY V.S. RAMACHANDRAN, 2011

"We are self-determined by the meaning we give to our experiences."

ALFRED ADLER

At the beginning of every year in elementary school, I told myself to practice nice handwriting. The new notebooks looked so nice, and their pages were so white, I wanted to keep them looking that way. I also decided to stay quiet and attentive. I saw myself being a "good boy" and I felt good seeing myself calm and appreciated. I didn't want to be sent home with a note from my teacher and have my mom or dad get upset at me and beat me because I was undisciplined. I knew in my head what it was to be "good." What puzzled me was that after a few weeks, I was "bad" again. My handwriting was all over the place, I couldn't understand what I wrote, I couldn't stand still and my grades went down. It pained me a lot, because

I wanted to come home with good grades. I wanted the teacher to like me and my parents to be proud of me. I wanted to be proud of me. I didn't want to be "the bad apple." I grew up believing that there was something wrong with me. I grew up second-guessing my words and actions; judging myself and others harshly.

Jane was a free spirited little girl; she was intelligent and had the capacity to see things as they were that went beyond her age. She knew what was fair or right immediately. Because of this, one time she questioned her mom's actions. Her father, a military man, stepped in and told the little girl in a stern way that in his house authority was not to be questioned. Jane "knew" that being herself was not ok. She tried hard to be a good girl and to do as she was supposed to do to gain love and acceptance. She learned to avoid conflict by not speaking her mind. Being helpful to others was an attempt to get the validation she always wanted, although her actions were not often recognized, making her resentful.

Helen was molested by a family friend when she was about four years old. When her mom found out, she told her that she was bad for allowing that man to touch her. Before this event took place, she was adored by her mom. She now feels that people judge and reject her constantly. Because of this, she is sensitive to people's actions and distrustful of people's intentions; she has become defensive and aggressive. Helen grew angry and judgmental, creating tense relationships in which she was always the victim of people's comments and intentions.

Although a single event may not be the only factor responsible for how we carry on with our lives, it could become the dominant factor around which we construct our beliefs, and consequently why we make it our life purpose to validate those beliefs. For Jane, expressing her beliefs and demanding what she wanted was not safe. She feared emotional pain, and she looked instead for approval and validation by helping others in the hope that she would be accepted and loved. Because the response to her actions didn't meet her emotional expectations, resentment was a constant part of her life, creating a circle of emotions in which she also felt unworthy of having her desires fulfilled.

As for me, I grew up believing that there was something wrong with me. Second-guessing my words and actions, judging myself and others harshly, limiting my actions in order to avoid encountering criticism or rejection, and isolating myself or limiting my contact with others lest they discover the "real," the "bad" me.

The reason why I started this book with bringing up these stories about early life events is because most of us have experienced, early in our lives, situations that created an impression so deep, that this new information overthrew and overshadowed all other events and memories in our lives. These experiences affect us so profoundly that we become reactive to events and to people in a way that is not consistent with how we envisioned ourselves acting and relating to them. Because we act with limited information, sometimes we do or say things that we clearly didn't intend to and walk away thinking, "What was I thinking when I said that, or acted that way?" It seems that just as we want to go right, an invisible force turns us left. It feels that although we are giving the commands and directions in our lives, we are not in the driver's seat. This driver goes wherever she wants with total disregard for our instructions or wishes. All kinds of life situations get affected by this, from small ones to big ones, from insignificant decisions we can't uphold to big ones in which at the last minute we do the unthinkable. *How can this happen, am I not in control of my life?*

When listening to my clients, I notice that somehow they have defined themselves in a narrow, manageable, easy-to-identify way for the most part. The severity of their inability to deal with reality could be traced back to how isolated the individual has been in her own analysis and interpretation of her memories, feelings and thoughts. In isolation, this is a never-ending process where there are thoughts about the previous thoughts and analysis of the previous analysis, all in all directed to validate their beliefs.

This may look like a very grim scenario with no way out, or at least that a very complex process is required to get out of this rut. However, the process is actually simpler than anything you may ever have done in the past. It will bring permanent changes in how you view, relate and experience reality. Therefore, you won't be reacting, but dynamically acting and engage in life.

Before getting there, we get to put some distance between those thoughts and beliefs, and ourselves. A pebble can make the whole world disappear if it's held close enough to our face. Although those events that distort reality amount to a small portion of our lives, just the same as with the pebble, they are perceived to be so close that we can't see or experience anything else. That is how we experience life. Our thoughts and beliefs become our whole and only reality, and we act accordingly. With no other alternative, we take refuge in what is familiar: the beliefs and thoughts that we have collected in the library of our mind for future reference. And referencing is all we do. That is what makes it difficult to reach an emotional balance. Using the information we already have is how we interpret our immediate reality. It makes it almost impossible to arrive at a new place if the information at hand is all about the old one.

Kim's father grew up in a culture where physical punishment was an acceptable way to discipline children. Her father hit her frequently; her mom was not emotionally available, and she was mainly attended to by her grandma.

For Kim, abuse was the norm. So, getting into an abusive relationship was understandable. She knew about these relationships, and they were familiar. She married twice, in both cases to abusive men. She got engaged to be married for the third time. This last relationship started failing when her grandmother, the only constant in her life, died. She became uneasy and distrusting, critical and hurtful towards her fiancé. Her fiancé was not an abusive man, he treated her with care. He was everything the others had not been. She became verbally abusive and she ended the relationship.

There is indeed an actual place, an alternate world, away from all the information we have accumulated throughout the years. A life that is more palpable and connected to reality, rather than to our thoughts.

You will find out the answer is simple, but not simplistic. You will need to do some work first before getting there. There is a reason why so many people have embarked themselves in developing theories and conducted research about the mind. The main purpose has been, and still is, to help us to have a choice and pursue what we really want in life.

It is very difficult to separate things in that closed environment that is our heads. It is as difficult as it would be to make a decision when you have two people screaming conflicting commands in each of your ears at all times. That is pretty much what goes on inside our heads all the time. How can we shut this noise off, so we are able to experience life clear of interference? There is no wonder why we make so many decisions we later regret.

Joe, a Marine, is in Iraq in 2003. A car with what appears to be locals inside is coming in the direction of his camp. He gives the order to have this car stopped and turned around, since this was a restricted area. One of the men speaking in his language seems to be complaining as the car continues to move slowly in their direction, ignoring the warnings. Knowing that other

American soldiers have been attacked and killed by people just like the people in the car, there was no way to know whether their intention would be the same. So as they inched closer, Joe gave the order to shoot at them. When Joe approached the car, he sees that one of the biggest bullets has taken the driver's head off, and in the back seat was a dead woman and the bodies of two little kids. He approached the surviving man and shot him in the head.

Shutting off the noise is what we are going to learn to do and it will be simple. I will repeat a lot of things throughout this book, so we can view and experience what our mind says from different angles without giving the obvious, logical or intellectual answer. The goal is for us to experience the information, internalizing it, so the understanding is not intellectual, but practical and experiential. Knowing intellectually doesn't equate to mastering the subject. I am aware that in one way or another you already know all that I will say in this book. I also know that if you are not in the driver's seat in some areas of your life, there is a need for mastery. Your intellectual understanding alone can't help you get what you really want.

What we find out about the above events is that the pain Joe experienced for the senseless death of the two little kids and the woman was unbearable to him since he was the one that gave the order to fire. To help him cope with the emotional pain, he turned to anger in order to mask it, authorizing himself to find the culprit, the cause for these events and the cause of his actions; it was war after all.

Shedding light on what has at some point been dark gives us the opportunity for choice. Without a choice we are powerless, we are blind in every aspect of our lives. Emotional distress affects everything in our lives. It handicaps us, prohibiting us from having intimate relationships or succeeding professionally and financially. It affects us spiritually because it may make everyone appear as our enemy. In darkness, everything seems to be only one thing, if we can't sort things out, there is nothing else to choose from.

The confusion that we live in is not entirely due to the events in our lives, but also the fact that they are intermingled with the vivid sounds, feelings, textures etc. of our memories and the thoughts we've had about those memories. The brain normal reaction to confusion and to what is unclear is fear; and fear we feel, fear we experience. Also, as our memories are replayed and relived, pain is experienced too. It is no wonder why we don't know the appropriate way to feel when we experience this melee of emotions and of memories that constantly jumps in unannounced. What is certain and ever-present is fear and pain, and avoiding these two becomes our life's purpose. These two have become our driver; life has become about protection. Going after what we want becomes secondary to avoiding fear and pain or the possibility of pain.

The goal is to bring simplicity to our thought processing so we can become functional, available. To depart from the convoluted intellectual processing of information and the automatic reaction when we feel emotionally threatened, and thus, to dive into experiencing life, to Being.

For a flying bird, understanding the physics of his flight and the mechanics of his movement in the air does not matter. What it does is fulfilling his nature, so he flies. We, like the bird, want to fulfill our true nature. We want to flap our wings and keep flying.

Whatever criteria for intelligence, one adopts purposeful groping, sudden comprehension or insight, coordination of means and ends, etc., everyone agrees in recognizing the existence of an intelligence before language. Essentially practical that is, aimed at getting results rather than stating truths. This intelligence nevertheless succeeds in eventually solving numerous problems of action (such as reaching distant or hidden objects) by constructing a complex system of action-schemes and organizing reality in terms of spatio-temporal and causal structures. In the absence of language or symbolic function, however, the constructions are made with the sole support of perceptions and movements and thus by means of a sensory-motor coordination of actions, without the intervention of representation or thought.

THE PSYCHOLOGY OF THE CHILD.
BY JEAN PIAGET & BARBEL INHELDER, 1966

TWO: Why is this book being written?

He took nothing for granted. He began a tradition of starting from scratch, assuming that the players were blank slates who carried over no knowledge from the year before... He began with the most elemental statement of all. "Gentlemen," he said, holding a pigskin in his right hand, "this is a football."

WHEN PRIDE STILL MATTERED: A LIFE OF
VINCE LOMBARDI
BY DAVID MARANISS, 1999

This book is about how to live a life of light of excitement with the same ease the brain has when it takes us to our darkest places, where we experience despair and hopelessness. This book is about experiencing life in the present.

This book's whole purpose is to present a lifetime of work discovering why we think the way we think, and consequently why we act the way we act. It is the result of a personal journey as well as the journey of my clients. This book is about understanding what gets in the way of the happiness we envision having, and the joy, creativity and the great relationships we want to have with ourselves and others. This book is about how to get there with the same ease the brain has when it takes us to our darkest places, where we experience despair and hopelessness. This book is about experiencing life in the present.

This book is not linear, although you may want it to be. It doesn't connect things as you are used to. It may upset you, an indication that it is stirring things up and challenging what you know. It repeats itself because that is what we do, that is how we learn.

I hope that by the end of this book you will have a different relationship with your brain, such that you can claim a reality that leaves you empowered to pursue a more engaging and fulfilling life. I hope you will be detached from the mostly useless information of the past, and cease projecting this information into the future, thus living in the present, engaged, in the zone, in the moment.

"Being depressed is not fun and the experience of it is even more depressing. And by being depressed I am not present, I am not aware of what is going on around me because I was so focused on what was making me depressed and how I was going to fix it, but I never did.

Thinking in Images has helped me not only to understand whatever situation I am in, whether I am depressed or happy or sad. It's helped me to be present; it helped me to be aware of what's going on. So now I am able to have a look at the big picture, understand it and move forward. Another example will be when I cleaned; I will clean until my fingers bleed. But why, I didn't know why then, but I know why now. I had to be in control. Being in control will somehow make me feel good about myself, but that wasn't reality. I wasn't present; I wasn't seeing it, I wasn't aware of what I was doing, but not anymore... I clean when I feel like it."

Francis

When there is no need for protection, possibilities are abundant. You can focus on relationships and pursue what you really want.

Over 35 years ago while attending business school, I sought out counseling with the resident psychologist and author Dr. Gustavo Adolfo Escobar Izasa. After a few sessions, he invited me to help him in a research he was conducting. I don't know exactly why he did it, maybe it was part of the therapy or because he actually saw some qualities in me that could be useful in his work. What I took from the whole experience was that I could conduct a research; that I was good enough and smart enough to figure things on my own. Well, the thought was not as apparent then as it was later in my life, but this was a window of hope into a balanced life away from irrational fears, and away from the prison of the mind. In the 1970's and early 80's, eating disorders, Asperger's syndrome, were not exactly well known topics for a therapist, much less in Colombia.

In my own search for answers, I continued my independent studies of psychology, and more significantly being psychoanalyzed and mentored by my new psychoanalyst, Dr. Jorge Victoria. This work went on for a period of 6 years, and as I was being psychoanalyzed, I worked with clients under Dr. Victoria's supervision. I also attended a series of transformational trainings and was trained as a Transformational Coach and Life Coach.

"The human individual, given a chance, tends to develop his particular human potentialities. He will then develop the unique alive forces of his real self: the clarity and depth of his own feelings, thoughts, wishes, interests; the ability to tap his own resources, the strength of his willpower; the special capacities or gifts he may have; the faculty to express himself, and to relate himself to others with his spontaneous feelings. In short, he will grow, substantially undiverted, toward self-realization."

The real self: "that central inner force, common to all human beings and yet unique in each, which is the deep source of growth."

To develop his given potentialities, one needs favorable conditions for growth: an atmosphere of warmth to give him both a feeling of inner security and the inner freedom, enabling him to have his own feelings and thoughts and to express himself. He needs the good will of others, not only to help him in his many needs, but to guide and encourage him to become a mature and fulfilled individual. Sometimes children grow up in environments where their elders are too wrapped up in their own neurosis to be able to love the child, or even to conceive of him as the particular individual he is. His elders may be dominating, overprotective, intimidating, irritable, over exacting, overindulgent, erratic, partial to other siblings, hypocritical, indifferent, etc.

As a result, the child does not develop a feeling of belonging, of "we," but instead a profound insecurity and vague apprehensiveness, or basic anxiety (the feeling of being isolated and helpless in a world conceived as potentially hostile). The cramping pressure of his basic anxiety prevents him from relating himself to others with the spontaneity of his real feelings, and forces him to find ways to cope with them. He must unconsciously deal with them in ways which do not arouse, or increase, but rather alleviate his basic anxiety.

He moves towards, against, or away from others: clings to the most powerful person; rebels and fights; tries to shut others out of his inner life and withdraw emotionally.

NEUROSIS AND HUMAN GROWTH: THE STRUGGLE TOWARD SELF-REALIZATION BY KAREN HORNEY, 1950

THREE: For whom is this book being written?

"A musician must make music, an artist must paint, a poet must write, if he is to be ultimately happy. What a man can be, he must be. This need we may call self-actualization."

A THEORY OF HUMAN MOTIVATION
BY ABRAHAM MASLOW, 1943

Psychoanalysis opened a lot of doors for me. "Every individual is a book on their own, as different from the next person as one novel is from the other," Dr. Victoria told me. A novel may have the same words as another, but it is still significantly different from any other, even if they tell the same history. Dr. Victoria was very strict about the dangers of projecting and reflecting my own thoughts, ideas, judgments, etc. on the clients. Because I was aware of my own narrative and how it could interfere with the comprehension of the client's nature and struggles, an important element was identified that has had a great impact in helping my clients and myself: the deconstruction of language.

When using language, we structure our communication building on the previous word or sentence we use while weaving a story. The emotional value we attach to our words depends on the emotional value the story has for us. This could lead to an exaggeration or over emphasizing of the emotional impact the events of the story had on us. Therefore, the events themselves get buried and often replaced by the story itself. Now, when the story is repeated it becomes consolidated in our minds as just the facts, rather than our personal experience of the facts. Deconstruction of the language, or bringing language and communication to its simplest form, helps the individual to distance him/herself from the series of interpretations/stories and the emotional value given to his/her life's events, mitigating the individual's conflicts enabling him/her to have a grasp on reality.

With this in mind and only an idea of a functional, self-sustaining individual, the theory evolved into a practice that in its simplest form makes sense to the senses. It enables the individual to create a life consistent with what he/she wants, transcending his/her perceived limitations. I called it, *Phroneidonics*, or *Thinking in Images*. *Thinking in Images* is something that we do naturally; it is what prompts us to action.

Phroneidonics: from the Greek word *phron* meaning thinking, *eido* meaning image, "that which is seen", and *ics* meaning principles, body of facts, knowledge.

Making the decision to recover was a difficult, complicated, and cognitive (intellectual) choice for me. On the one hand, I loved the bliss of drifting in the current of the eternal flow. Who wouldn't? It was beautiful there. My spirit beamed free, enormous, and peaceful. In the rapture of an engulfing bliss, I had to question what recovery really meant. Clearly, there were some advantages to having a functional left hemisphere... Honestly, there were certain aspects of my new existence that I preferred over the way I had been before. I was not willing to compromise my new insights in the name of recovery. I liked knowing I was a fluid. I loved knowing my spirit was at one with the universe and in the flow with everything around me. I found it fascinating to be so tuned into energy dynamics and body language. But most of all, I loved the feeling of deep inner peace that flooded the core of my very being.

I yearned to be in a place where people were calm and valued my experience of inner peace. Because of my heightened empathy, I found that I was overly sensitive to feeling other people's stress. If recovery meant that I had to feel like they felt all the time, I wasn't interested. It was easy for me to separate my "stuff" and emotions from other people's "stuff" and emotions by choosing to observe but not engage. As Marianne Williamson puts it, "Could I rejoin the rat race without becoming a rat again?"

MY STROKE OF INSIGHT, A BRAIN SCIENTIST'S PERSONAL JOURNEY
BY JILL BOLTE TAYLOR, PH.D. 2008

We all know the concepts regarding what it takes to live a proactive life of connection. We have read enough to be able to "intellectually" understand how to live a successful life. And yet we still "don't know" how to get there. How is this possible? For many of my clients, it takes them only a short amount of time to overcome their limitations and experience a fuller life and a life of engagement. What this means is that they have been able to detach from who they think they are, freeing them to experience a life that is outside of the Identity they have co-created with their mind, and which so far has been the only reality available; the reality of the Identity we call "me." It is now clear to me that *Thinking in Images* is a way to rapidly become available to having the kind of life we know is possible for us.

I define Identity as everything that the stories of my experiences are comprised of, the emotional value I place on those experiences, all my beliefs about everything I experience, and everything I call and believe to be "me."

I use the terms brain, mind, and *Identity* interchangeable; I am referring to the function they do organizing and interpreting external stimulus, assessing and categorizing reality.

FOUR: How is this Book Being Written?

"However much we champion freedom of thought, we actually spend much of our time censoring input. We seek out publications that mirror or support our prior views and largely avoid those that don't."

DECEIT AND SELF-DECEPTION: FOOLING YOURSELF THE BETTER TO FOOL OTHERS BY ROBERT TRIVERS, 2011.

The principles and practice in the following chapters are not designed to appeal to your intellect. Your intellect has brought you only this far. It probably makes you a great professional and successful person. But when it comes to the depths of you, your spirit, your essence, your being, "it," your intellect can't have you experience what you yearn for—achieving this means that you must transcend intellectual thought. It is the experience, not just the thought of the experience, that I aim to help you find through this work. And I invite you, as successful as you might be, to embrace the idea that there could be new things to discover and further growth and expansion to achieve. I deliberately use a simple language that doesn't comprise any profound intellectual thought processing, and I invite you to let yourself go and float on the words.

For example, if I were to ask you, "Does this make sense to you?" the answer would be, "Yes, it makes sense. It feels right, but I don't understand." And that will be ok. Your understanding has been your filter throughout your life experiences. This is an invitation to freedom. To experience life free of intellectual thought, free of filters. The purpose of *Thinking in Images: The Path to Being* is to help you realize who you are not, so you can embark on a lifelong journey of discovery, so you can create meaningful relationships, and be engaged in everyday life. It is not to feed the intellect, but to profoundly realize our relationship with our minds and alter it so that we are able to be present at all moments.

Love touched the hearts of the Brahmans' young daughters when Siddhartha walked through the lanes of the town with the luminous forehead, with the eye of a king, with his slim hips. But more than all the others, he was loved by Govinda, his friend, the son of a Brahman... he loved everything Siddhartha did and said and what he loved most was his spirit, his transcendent, fiery thoughts, his ardent will, his high calling... Siddhartha was thus loved by everyone. He was a source of joy to everybody, he was a delight to them all. But he, Siddhartha, was not a source of joy to himself, he found no delight in himself. Walking the rosy paths of the fig tree garden, sitting in the bluish shade of the grove of contemplation, washing his limbs daily in the bath of repentance, sacrificing in the dim shade of the mango forest, his gestures of perfect decency, everyone's love and joy, he still lacked all joy in his heart. Dreams and restless thoughts came into his mind, flowing from the water of the river, sparkling from the stars of the night, melting from the beams of the sun, dreams came to him and a restlessness of the soul... Siddhartha had started to nurse discontent in himself, he had started to feel that the love of his father and the love of his mother, and also the love of his friend, Govinda, would not bring him joy forever and ever, would not nurse him, feed him, satisfy him... the vessel was not full, the spirit was not content, the soul was not calm, the heart was Siddhartha: The ablutions were good, but they were water, they did not wash off the sin, they did not heal the spirit's thirst, they did not relieve the fear in his heart...where, where was this self, this innermost part, this ultimate part? It was not flesh and bone, it was neither thought, nor consciousness, thus the wisest ones taught. So, where, where was it? To reach this place, the self, myself, the Real Self, there was another way, which was worthwhile looking for? Alas, and nobody showed this way, nobody knew it, not the father, and not the teachers and wise men, not the holy sacrificial songs! ... Surely, many verses of the holy books spoke of this innermost and ultimate thing, wonderful verses. "Your soul is the whole world," was written there, and it was written that man in his sleep, in his deep sleep, would meet with his innermost part and would reside in the Real Self. —But where were the... wise men or penitents, who had succeeded in not just knowing this deepest of all knowledge but also to live it? Where was the knowledgeable one who wove his spell to bring his familiarity with the Real Self out of the sleep into the state of being awake, into the life, into every step of the way, into word and deed? ...The Son of the Brahman many venerable Brahmans, chiefly his father, the pure one, the scholar, the most venerable one. His father was to be admired, quiet and noble were his manners, pure his life, wise his words, delicate and noble thoughts lived behind its brow —but even he, who knew so much, did he live in blissfulness, did he have peace, was he not also just a searching man, a thirsty man? Did he not, again and again, have to drink from holy sources, as a thirsty man, from the offerings, from the books, from the disputes of the Brahman? Why did he, the irreproachable one, have to wash off sins every day, strive for a cleansing every day, over and over every day? Was not the Real Self in him, did not the pristine source spring from his heart? It had to be found, the pristine source in one's own self, it had to be possessed! Everything else was searching, was a detour, was getting lost. Thus were Siddhartha's thoughts, this was his thirst, this was his suffering.

SIDDHARTHA
BY HERMANN HESSE, 1922

FIVE: How to Read this Book and What to Expect

"I have been and still am a seeker, but I have ceased to question stars and books; I have begun to listen to the teaching my blood whispers to me."

DEMIAN: THE STORY OF EMIL SINCLAIR'S
YOUTH
BY HERMANN HESSE, 1963

The way to read this book is not trying to memorize any of its parts. Let it represent any part of your life. Unobtrusively it will start to alter your relationship with the reality you have lived up to now, opening the doors to the Being, to the other you, the one without hesitation; because this "you" acts on the conviction and the evidence that things are possible. Here we relate with facts with clear awareness of our emotions about those facts, thus we are not hijacked by our emotions. Interestingly here we are, more compassionate and empathetic because we are less judgmental; no longer referencing everyone against our memories and the emotions we felt in the past.

I invite you to steer away from finding the answer, or trying to figure out what to do next in order to fix things. Things will come together automatically and you will start to experience a clarity that was elusive before. It is not a miracle cure, it will require practice and we will present the practice later on. The more patient and willing you are to be comfortable with the uncomfortableness of not knowing, the more capable you are to avoid the rush to get "there," the more profoundly affected your view of the world and yourself will be and the more permanent the changes will be.

We are throwing a monkey wrench into the machinery that has governed your world, feeding you the information that tells you your options are limited. The information that commands you with "shoulds" and "should nots," without any evidence of what is possible in the present moment.

Michael, a 70-year-old man, has been depressed all his life. He had been medicated for years to help him control his depression and suicidal thoughts. Highly sensitive to criticism or anything he perceived as such, his relationships with his siblings were delicate, and he always looked for attention and validation, attention that others felt as an imposition. Although a man 70 years of age, he still experienced life as if he had no say in it. Others were to be blamed for his feelings of rejection and disapproval. He felt rejected and judged, and he blamed it on being gay and being different. Although there were changes around him, nothing changed inside of him. He still judged others and himself harshly. His beliefs were his only reality. This manifested itself in demands others could not fulfill, and sometimes caused people to react aggressively, validating his own thoughts about himself and others.

He came to realize that he only made choices with the limited information he had, and that he was not aware of any reality other than the one he had experience all his life. Once he realized and was aware that the chatter he heard in his mind wasn't his own, he started to experienced a sense of freedom. He came to realize the freedom he had without the judgments that had him pinned down to his beliefs. He was able to make a radical distinction between the reality of his thoughts and the present moment, thus helping him to start developing a new system with the new information. Now he experiences life and is aware of the thoughts of the old system of the Identity, and follows the choices that are consistent with the life he now wants to experience. Thinking in Images allows him not to fall into the narratives that in the past controlled his thoughts and created a life of resentment.

In his own words: "I do experience faintly the feelings I felt in the past like a distant voice and yet I don't engage with them. I am not medicated anymore. Never before have I experienced this freedom, in which I am the one choosing at all times."

Information is just stored data. Think of all the family movies, the not-so-family movies and photos, and add all your thoughts about those movies to it. Although a memory begins with perception—all we see, smell, and feel, it is encoded and stored using electricity and chemicals. Here's how it works. Nerve cells connect with other cells at a point called a synapse. All the action in your brain occurs at these synapses, where electrical pulses carrying messages leap across gaps between cells. The electrical firing of a pulse across the gap triggers the release of chemical messengers called neurotransmitters. These neurotransmitters diffuse across the spaces between cells, attaching themselves to neighboring cells. Each brain cell can form thousands of links like this, giving a typical brain about 100 trillion synapses. The parts of the brain cells that receive these electric impulses are called dendrites, feathery tips of brain cells that reach out to neighboring brain cells. This is how the brain is "replaying" and/or "recording" memories/information.

The connections between brain cells aren't set in concrete -- they change all the time. It all depends on how often we use this information (how often we think these thoughts). Brain cells work together in a network, organizing themselves into groups that specialize in different kinds of information processing. As one brain cell sends signals to another, the synapse between the two gets stronger. It has to do with how often this information is accessed. The more signals sent between them, the stronger the connection grows. Thus, **with each new experience, your brain slightly rewires its physical structure.** In fact, how you use your brain helps determine how your brain is organized. It is this flexibility, which scientists call plasticity, that can help your brain rewire itself.

Almost 10 years after the decision to write this book, the language in which I wanted to write started to take form. Two years ago after a lot of working and writing, I found a narrative that I felt comfortable with, and little by little it became the language that didn't make me cringe when I read it.

It is a narrative and language that was close to the one I use with my clients and that has been proven to be very effective.

As I read one of the sections, I saw in front of me what I was looking for. A narrative that felt comfortable and that was consistent with the work I do with my clients. I felt a sense of accomplishment after years of continuous work and fearing the possibility of not finding what I was looking for. This was a great feeling. Without realizing it, the main body of the book was already finished, with the exception of certain stories and excerpts from a few scientists and philosophers that needed to be included. My friend Joe Palmer has helped me to organize the book into sections, something that gave me a view of the entirety of the work and brought fluidity to the whole book.

The section that had brought the most feelings of accomplishments, I wanted to share with my sister, someone I respect. But something really interesting started to develop. I started to dislike what I wrote. *"It's not going to make sense, it sounds like blah-blah, it's worthless,"* I thought. All the voices and thoughts of rejection in my head were getting really loud. I am familiar with these thoughts as they have been there all along during these 10 years. The way I coped with them was getting sleepy, finding things to do that were more immediate than writing, and telling myself that I needed more time to be able to communicate better. Avoiding the people that will and "are" rejecting me was important. I didn't want to go through that fear and that pain so I stalled.

But this time, I wasn't stalling.

It became apparent that my experience of the book changed from one day to the other.

I revised the sections, printed it, revised it again, printed again. I did this several times.

How is it possible to feel this way about something that previously I liked so much? But that was an afterthought. Now I was scared.

The day came, and I gave my sister the printed section. She read it and then she said, "I like the way you used the examples to explain the big concepts, it makes it so simple to visualize them."

The incredible thing was that not only did I start to like my work again, but my mind felt clearer and more creative now.

Before, these emotions went unquestioned and I acted or reacted accordingly. I just felt the emotions and without questioning them, I filled in the blanks with what I had in front of me. I took many detours in my life, stopped many ideas from being realized and hurt people on account of these kinds of thoughts and emotions; all caused by the beliefs I held.

This process, the *Thinking in Images Process*, is not about smoothing the edges of our personality. Personality, *Identity* is what we create as a response to threats, and it is consolidated by our relationships with our parents, close relatives, culture, etc. Thinking in Images is about distancing ourselves from that persona that we have identified ourselves with, thus debilitating the old system and creating a new system with the information that will allow us to experience the life we really want.

That has been the quest all along, not only for me, but for many other people: How can I experience life differently? Do I have any control over my thoughts, and if not can I learn a way to do it? It was disheartening not to have an alternative to that grim, dark, inescapable reality. I knew it would take me many years to discover a way out, let alone an effective and permanent one.

However, the fact that I took refuge in my mind created a unique way of experiencing life for me, since my perception of it was altered by my fears and my need for protection. The outcome was the feeling that I was not experiencing life as it was, but as I allowed it to be. Colors were not as bright, and I perceived people as being separate from me, as if I were watching them on TV. They were different, not a part of my life, and yet they were in it. The feelings I experienced by seeing them interact, so friendly and casual with each other, sometimes even touching one another or leaning on each other, were those of bewilderment, sadness, confusion, guilt.

Judgments started to form. I needed something that could help me make sense of what I was witnessing and experiencing. Then the thought occurred. There must be something wrong with me. I felt that I did not belong here. They were speaking in a language that I did not understand, but I wanted to. The spiraling downward fall from my understanding was a huge leap from reality. Although I could help people make sense of their life, I could not experience mine. How could I know and yet not know?

So I chose to help people, vicariously helping myself. I read and studied a lot; not looking for a magical answer, just a simple one. But then after years of fighting, of working, of darkness, it all started to come together. All the concepts and the practices started to align, creating a bundled solution that worked. I had found a sequence that sheds light on the darkness, and is a pathway to a full life, peace and genesis of creation. My motivation was that I wanted to see life with real colors instead of the fuzzy images that I was witnessing. My mind was producing so many thoughts so fast that they blurred reality, leaving me trapped inside my head, only experiencing life through the eyes of others. This was the closest thing to reality for me. It is difficult to explain, but the colors and shapes were not sharp. It was as if I was looking at the world through a screen. It took me years to experience life outside of my own thoughts and to see the real colors of life, to figure it out. And this was not figuratively—when the "sound" of my thoughts quieted, the colors of things become literally more vivid, the lines of things more defined, and l could see more things; I became aware of a world much richer and brighter that the one my mind had created.

My life as I experienced it was extremely complex and difficult all because I couldn't relate and be close to people as I saw other people do. Social settings are an unpredictable space, and I was not aware that often when I was not controlling the conversation, my mind left the room. Later I found out that people felt offended by this, concluding that my demeanor was of superiority. Also, when people were talking, I was staring at them intently, diving into their words and believing anything that I was told. It was so fascinating seeing other people being normal, human, social beings playing the social game, something that was so foreign to me. Honestly, it is still to some degree difficult for me. I have to remind myself to stay present, and not retreat into my world of thoughts in order to be more comfortable.

It was a very interesting journey in which claiming my humanity was a very long quest. I had to understand and accept the desire to belong and to be social, and the limitation and the lack of endurance required to successfully keep my relationships, to find my limits for social activity.

I have spent over 40 years looking for a way to bypass the thought-producing-mind and exploring other possible, more fulfilling realities. I had a sense that the mind was a foreign object, but 40 years ago I would have been categorized as crazy for saying this. Plus the influence of culture and my own readings didn't allow this thought to exist out in the open. It only existed as an anomaly that needed to be suppressed or destroyed. The cost of expressing it would be becoming a social outcast, and I had a desire to fit in—to be "normal."

What I later found out was that I'm not broken, and that there isn't anything wrong with the way I am. I am just different, and the people I work with, my clients, and everyone around me is just fine. There is nothing wrong with them. It's just how we view ourselves that makes us wrong. The big conflict appears when we try to turn ourselves somehow into the idea we have of how we should be. Then the simple becomes complex, and access to our abilities to perform, to relate becomes limited. We want to be friendly and yet any little thing makes us defensive, even aggressive. We shy away from being assertive in the workplace or in our relationships, and we give up on pursuing our passions for fear of rejection.

This whole work is to put in people's hands simple tools for them to manifest the uniqueness that they are; not in terms of their appearance or beliefs, but their real essence, being played out in the space of Being and not in the space of thought. This saves them from any diagnosis that the expert may formulate as a way for the expert to have a better intellectual grasp of something that seems to have too many moving parts. Believing that the expert's job is to alleviate the symptoms and to feed the client a normalized life, the solution the expert usually presents will create other conflicts and will deprive the individual of their unique way of looking at the world, affecting creativity, problem solving, and the ability to achieve an elevated state of Being.

In the process of developing this theory and practice, I decided years ago to stop reading anything pertaining to the mind and start exploring on my own. Therefore, I arrived at conclusions that other people had found either earlier or later. I will mention some of these individuals at some point in the book by quoting them for those of you that would like to explore the subject further. These scientists are not the only the ones that are doing the work, but they communicate in a clearer and more compelling way the works of the mind that are referenced in *Thinking in Images*.

To get the best out of this book, you must not worry about what it is that you are getting from reading it, or storing the information for later referencing. Actually, that probably would be your worst enemy in the process of learning about yourself. So, don't worry about keeping track of what you are learning, or taking any detailed notes. If you pick up the book and open it to a random page, you will always experience it in new ways. The information won't change, but your experience will if you allow yourself to experience it in your new and present context. I guarantee you will learn something different. Experiencing things anew is how wisdom occurs and manifests.

The excerpts that I include are to support and complement your own analysis. Certainly, this is included for the nerd in you, but also to support the creation of the new system. However, if you want the full impact of this work in your life, skip the excerpts that you don't enjoy and only go back to them when what you have read has affected the way you respond to the experiences in your life.

If you have the need to read it, go ahead and do it. Just be aware and notice that your mind has the need for the security of understanding intellectually. This is just fine. Just notice, and be in contact with what your mind is doing.

Trust that you will rediscover the essence of you, and in that space the right words, answers and actions will be available to you so you can create a life worth living.

The objective is to come to the profound realization that we are not the movie playing our heads.

SIX: From Complex to Simple

"In truth, when we set out to explain our actions, they are all post hoc, after the fact, explanations using after the fact observation with no access to nonconscious processing. Not only that, our left brain fudges, alters things a bit to fit into a make-sense story."

WHO'S IN CHARGE? FREE WILL AND THE
SCIENCE OF THE BRAIN
BY MICHAEL S. GAZZANIGA, 2011

I liked to listen to my dad's stories. I listened to and lived every detail of them. I was sixteen when he told me the story of how when he was fifteen, he had to take his dad to a faraway place because he had Hansen's Disease, or dry leprosy. In 1929 lepers, people with this disease were confined to a place far from everyone's contact, by law. My dad was so detailed in his story, I saw him disappear into his tale. "I had to say goodbye to him at a gate, I saw my dad walk away." As my dad, a sixty-year-old man was telling me this story with tears rolling down his wrinkled face, I only could see and experience a boy of sixteen years old.

Indeed, at that moment, he was a fifteen-year-old boy and not my dad anymore.

It was puzzling to see how the mind can be so far removed from reality as to cause us to flee the present moment and travel decades to a memory that completely erased all awareness of the context and the content of our present lives and who we have become. I myself was sharing this reality, and despite the wrinkled face, I was in the presence of a boy and I experienced the pain of seeing him waving goodbye to his dad.

If it was possible to abandon my reality and to exist in his, and for him to escape his to travel back in time, would it be possible to exist at will in the reality of our choosing, away from the frightening thoughts that pin us down and give us no choice but to hide out in fear?

This was a wall that I was just staring at, but wanted to climb. Somehow I believed that on the other side I could find the answers to my own thoughts and anguish.

To be *Thinking in Images*, to Be, to experience the present, we first have to understand the complexity of what we have created as our reality and why we have created it. The intellectual process that we have used up to now to interpret reality rather than experiencing it is convoluted, and it requires an endless string of thoughts to fill in the gaps, inconsistencies in our experiences, and interpretations of our experiences in order to validate our opinions, beliefs and expectations.

The goal is to depart from this way of thinking, since this is why we experience life as we do and the consequent anguish that comes with it.

The question is how to be functional without losing our uniqueness, our humanity.

This is the delicate path we take in *Thinking in Images* – figuring out how to depart from our *Identity* without becoming cynical about the emotions we have created, so we can enjoy and connect with art, with stories and with others on an emotional level.

As I was growing up, I noticed that people exist in the narrative of their own mind, and the stories they create take the place of real life. We string words together, creating a narrative that once initiated requires more narratives to support and validate the previous proposition or statement.

Once we start a story, we will say almost anything to support it. The more important the story or the audience or need to be accepted and validated, the more we are willing to add to it, even if it is half-truth or not true at all.

Have you ever told a story and found that as you were telling it, you knew you were making up things as you went, but you just couldn't shut up, so you just kept going?

Language at this point becomes the obstacle to Being. Once the events have already occurred, we confine them to memory along with what we feel and think about them, creating the narratives about those events. These narratives will be the information we will access once those memories are triggered. We now are experiencing life through our narratives.

Narratives get richer with time as we remember them or relate them to others, making them more vivid and attaching more feelings to them.

Narratives become our only reality, and they take the place of the actual events. Events as they actually happen are no longer relevant.

This process is not about understanding intellectually how to land in the present. You have read enough and have enough knowledge to do that. If you let yourself be in the "I don't understand, but it makes sense," you will be learning to experience life from Being instead of only experiencing the thoughts your mind feeds you.

If you have done any kind introspection or reading with the purpose of appeasing your mind, you know how to get there and probably have been there at least once. You probably have experienced, if even for a nanosecond, the peace, the joy, and the profound understanding of things as if you understood the Whole, and you became one with the Whole.

And yet you did not really fully understand it, because when we try to understand it with our intellect, we want it to make sense as a progression does. The problem is the way we learned to process information, in a linear and sequential way. However, the kind of understanding required to Being is quite different. Here we are in contact with the whole without a need for a specific answer. Specific answers are needed to perform tasks, they are not needed to *Be*. When we are Being, we just *Be*. A specific answer will disconnect us from the whole and shift our focus to the specific.

I didn't set any premise for *Thinking in Images*, instead, I just followed; I observed and followed the ideas and my clients' evolution. I didn't want this work to be the reflection of my own limitations and consequently have to force ideas that may not be suitable to achieving the result I was looking for. I was looking for a way to experience life away from all the information the brain has gathered and all its warnings, to explore life as it is and be engaged with everyone, to experience belonging, to submit oneself to life, and to just *Be*.

The work of *Thinking in Images, The Path to Being* is not about finding who you are. This thing, this *me* that I created is what has tainted life, making it something that it is not. To the contrary, this work is about how to relinquish "me." It is about discovering life away from whom you made yourself believe you were, to be free to experience *Being*. Being is to be in action and being in action is to live in the present.

Thinking in Images is an action. It is a way to experience life as the phrase states it: *in Images*, rather than in words. It is experiencing life as being part of the whole and using information/*Identity*, to create and to transcend, instead of giving it the task of interpreting emotional reality for us.

Thinking in Images is a "*Path to Being*," it is a path in which we surrender our *Identity*, and we free ourselves of the boundaries of the information we have accumulated throughout our lives, allowing us to experience the whole. *Thinking in Images, The Path to Being* enables us to create a new relationship with our brain where reality is experienced and not thought about.

We will come to the realization that the mind acts independently, and that we have been listening to this information as if it was generated by us. How can we not, when it is inside of us? We act in life as if every piece of information the mind provides is real, and therefore we become co-producers of our personal movie with that information.

Thinking in Images is a process designed to be unobtrusive, delivered in a way that is ordinary, creating a context in which the individual is willing to step out and separate from her *Identity*, allowing her to experience herself away from the preconceived "knowledge" of reality and the predictable future.

Thinking in Images is the deconstruction of the *Identity*. It identifies the complex building that the mind has created, giving it an intellectual stronghold on reality. This process can be very challenging and scary. These structures, this building, this *Identity* and our beliefs are the only reality that gives us "security" in the beginning, and the only one we know, or perhaps choose to know. Realizing the nature of this building and complex structure will bring into awareness and put at our disposal the possibility of diving into the pool of Being, an alternative reality to that of our thoughts. Freedom from our *Identity* as the only reality can allow us to manifest our wants through willful actions, engagement and availability to possibilities other than what our mind, in its need to protect, present us.

Even the name of this book didn't come upuntil about nine years ago. In the early stages, there was a very broad set of principle and concepts, and the horizon looked somewhat fuzzy, but the feeling was that I was heading in the right direction given the response my clients had to this work. Even then, I knew that I didn't have a complete grasp and understanding of some of its parts.

As the work continued, things became clearer, the concepts more precise and crisp. Therefore, I feel comfortable now presenting *Thinking in Images* in the form of this book; although it is not the whole theory, because there are elements that need to be explored that are more profound. This will be done with subsequent writings, but the basis of the theory is present in this book. The reader should be able to apply these concepts in his/her life and benefit from them immediately.

I will describe in a general way, enough for the reader to have an idea of how it is that the brain works, and for him/her to have a pivot point at which to launch him/her into this journey of discovery and depart from the ideas that used to govern his/her reality, causing him/her anguish and despair.

Life is happening right now and is in limited supply since it will come to an abrupt end at some point. We can't possibly know at what moment this experience we call reality will be no more, and yet we all to some degree live it as if it can be saved for a later moment, at which time we will be fully engaged. We all fantasize about the things we want to do, and we promise that we will do them when the conditions are ideal, but the ideal conditions never come together.

The fear of pain and the experience of fear itself is enough for us to become separate, building this unique "me" that has everything figured out, that will watch over us.

By doing so, we suffocate our Being and we exchange it for guaranteed information and understanding. We create an *Identity* that will negotiate life for us. We exchange experiencing life for the information about life. We become separate because belonging does not give us control. In belonging, there is no way to predict the outcome. In belonging, we are vulnerable. What this means is we are open to experiencing the whole, including pain and fear.

Not allowing people to go through their pain, and protecting them from it, may turn out to be a kind of over-protection, which in turn implies a certain lack of respect for the integrity and the intrinsic nature and the future development of the individual.

TOWARD A PSYCHOLOGY OF BEING
BY ABRAHAM MASLOW, 1962

It is pretty scary to abandon one's *Identity*, the one I "know" as myself. We don't realize that in belonging, all is about "me"; however, the experience of it escapes our intellectual understanding. We want the certainty of intellectual understanding, and the collection of information we can reference that makes the world predictable.

Societies would not be better off if everyone were like Mr. Spock, all rationality and no emotion. Instead, a balance—a teaming up of the internal rivals—is optimal for brains. ... Some balance of the emotional and rational systems is needed, and that balance may already be optimized by natural selection in human brains.

INCOGNITO: THE SECRET LIVES OF THE
BRAIN
BY DAVID EAGLEMAN, 2011

SEVEN: Packing for Your Journey

I confused things with their names: that is belief.

THE WORDS: THE AUTOBIOGRAPHY OF JEAN-
PAUL SARTRE
BY JEAN-PAUL SARTRE, 1963

It is very difficult to separate things in that closed environment that is our heads. It is as difficult as it would be to make a decision when you have two people screaming conflicting commands in each of your ears at all times.

Right in this moment, you have a movie playing inside your head. It is the most complex movie you have ever heard of because it looks, feels, and smells like reality. It plays out our memories and scenes from our childhood, and of course, we experience them as if we are there in that moment with its entire array of emotions and feelings.

This movie is actually a collage of movies that were shot early in our lives, and when it is playing, it takes us back to those smells, pains, fears and faces. This movie feels and tastes like reality, and in the theater of our mind, it is real. Therefore, it's no wonder that the reality outside this theater of the mind is experienced as not real, or at least not as real as the one that is crowding our senses. The reality in the theater of the mind is reality for us, and what is outside of it is incorporated into its storyline, so it makes sense to us to create a unified universe. The only universe we are aware of most of the time.

Philosophy Professor John Searle at USC Berkeley doesn't like the movie metaphor because… "that suggest there is a distinction between the movie and the guy watching the movie. And that is not true, we are the movie," – he said.

I believe that he is right. When we experience the movie with no awareness or distinction that it is a movie, we become the fulfillment of the movie, we are being the movie.

Dr. B, was at a department store somehow agitated because his demands had not been met, or so he thought. The customer service representative, a mature woman, told him to sit down and wait until she figured out what the problem was. He found himself, to his surprise, telling the lady she was not his mom and demanding his needs be met immediately.

His relationship at the moment was not with the lady in front of him, but with the movie starting to play inside his brain. His brain probably referenced his mom, who was a dominant woman, and as soon as he saw the customer service lady, he projected her into the scene, assuming that she was in control and that he was powerless—just as in the movie the brain shot long ago.

For some, what triggers the movies are their moms, dads, brothers or sisters, teachers, bullies, war, etc. The reality is that these faces and events keep overriding reality, making us a little or a lot more jumpy in response to the events at hand.

Peter B: I went to visit my childhood friend Bill and for the first time in the last, I don't know, six times the conversation was not a downer or depressing, even though he is having marriage problems. It seems that all the people coming to his shop kind of distracted him.

Alberto: Sometimes, maybe most of the time, we believe that things happen to us randomly and we just happen to be there on the receiving end with no contribution to the events.

Often we fail to see the contribution we give to people's lives. Given that your meetings with Bill have been consistently full of depressing exchanges, and the fact that you now have a different relationship with your life, it is possible that you may have directly affected the outcome of this last meeting. You are either validating the *Identity* or developing yourself away from it.

Let me illustrate how we contribute and affect the outcome in relationships with an example:

Imagine that you are walking and in the distance, you see someone walking in your direction. As you see this person approach you, you seem to anticipate that this person has ill-intentions and she is going to do or say something rude to you. And you were right, as you crossed paths she looked at you aggressively and with disgust.

Maybe this person indeed has something affecting her. As you imagine that you were the subject of her thoughts, you probably got ready and your body language was representing your thoughts. We don't know for sure what was going on in her mind, but we know that you were physically prepared.

Now let's look at the situation from the other perspective, her perspective. She sees a man who is intently looking at her and seems to be tense and somehow aggressive, and she gets defensive. As a way to keep him at bay, she looks at him defiantly.

Let's go a little further and imagine that she is just immersed in her own thoughts, and you are having a challenging day. Because of this, you may be feeling vulnerable and sensitive to rejection. It is possible that you will project your own thoughts on the people around you without being conscious of it. This is what we do most of the time when we see aggression in most people's actions, causing us to prepare to defend or even attack before we are attacked.

Now let's go back to the first example in which you are preparing for an attack. You perceive rejection because you believe the woman looks aggressive. You are ready, your body obviously will be tense; and as she comes close to you, she smiles. The object of your tension and your thoughts is not being supported. The feeling you get could be confusion, feeling silly, relief, happy, or maybe all of these.

Now let's go back again to the first example, and let's assume that she indeed is projecting her own problems on you, but this time you don't prepare yourself and instead when the two of you cross paths, you smile.

We don't know for sure what the outcome will be, but certainly, either way, we are influencing the space in which we choose to show up, and knowing what we bring may be the ticket to our freedom of self-expression. It will take for you to be aware, just aware of what you bring. Don't judge it, just look at it and notice it.

This *Identity* is the one playing the movies, and once it senses something remotely threatening, it immediately accesses the archives of the mind, it rummages through all the information we have accumulated and plays the bit that references the experience and emotions we are having and most of the time embellishes it, with our help, of course.

Deconstructing language

Without the support of language and its infinite string of narratives, stories and the emotional value we attach to them, we get closer to the events, experiencing emotions that are connected to the facts rather than fabricated emotions that are related to thoughts and beliefs we co-created with our *Identity*.

Language is built by connecting words in a narrative, the more creative the individual, the richer in words and subtleties the narration will be. It depends on the emotional impact the events may have had on the individual. The greater the impact, the more emotional value will be attached to the words.

We seldom say, "I am hurt," and leave it at that. If we could say just that and experience just that emotion, pain, we would still be available to everything at the moment. However, there is always an explanation attached to it. As we explain our emotions we put more words into the story, the emotional value increases and we abandon reality and fall deep into our story. The emotional sting associated with that story is what we will remember as reality.

...The real problem is not to locate the first appearance of intelligence, but rather to understand the mechanism of this progression. For many psychologists, this mechanism is one of association, a cumulative process by which conditionings are added

to reflexes and many other acquisitions to the conditionings themselves. According to this view, every acquisition, from the simplest to the most complex, is regarded as a response to external stimuli, response whose associative character expresses a complete control of development by external connections. One of us, on the other hand, has argued that this mechanism consists in assimilation (comparable to biological assimilation in the broad sense): meaning that reality data are treated or modified in such a way as to become incorporated into the structure of the subject. In other words, every newly established connection is integrated into an existing schematism.

THE PSYCHOLOGY OF THE CHILD BY JEAN PIAGET AND BARBEL INHELDER, 1969

Someone may attend a party and in the first three hours have a great time, dance, laugh, and have great connections and conversations. At this time, someone drops a glass of wine on them, staining their clothes. The person may say, "My whole party was ruined, I knew it was too good to be true."

The memory we create of the event becomes the relevant information that is stored and not the actual events. This information is what the brain will access in the future to reference. A simple way of putting it, when the individual is having a great time he/she will listen to the warning of the brain and will be on the lookout for something going wrong and anything that may fit that description will be blown out of proportion to validate that belief. If you are the one in a relationship with someone that believes that something always ruins the time they are having, you may be the one that will present the validation for that belief. If on the other hand, you are the one with the belief, your partner is the one that will become the subject of your misery.

Remember Jane the free spirited little girl with the military father?

Jane went to marry a man that was in great contrast with her dad. Mike was patient, and gave her freedom to do as she pleased. At the beginning of their marriage, they shared a lot and did things together. Jane, a professional, started to spend more time at work. This is how she felt validated; she took on more than she was supposed to, and she did this for years. Mike didn't complain, granting her the space to be, so with time he engaged himself in activities on his own.

Now Jane is 52 years old and thinking of the possibility of life alone since she doesn't experience the relationship working. She now wants to experience more, try new restaurants, have conversations with her husband, and she wants to travel. Mike fell into his own pace after more than 25 years of Jane doing what she at the time wanted.

We have a great investment in the reality we have created, and the reality we have streamlined that makes sense to us is vital. It is what gives us a sense of placement in our particular group, in life and in general. This reality has been figured out with the goal of shielding us from the dangers the brain constantly warns us about; that past events will repeat themselves and that we may or will experience pain. The mind/*Identity* will concoct any kind of story to protect the integrity of what we came to believe is reality.

"I believe that things just happen in life, and pretty much after the fact, we make up a story to make it all seem rational. We all like simple stories that suggest a causal chain to life's events. Yet randomness is ever present."

TALES FROM BOTH SIDES OF THE BRAIN: A
LIFE IN NEUROSCIENCE
BY MICHAEL S. GAZZANIGA, 2015

The brain's thought processing, its referencing, the automatic conclusions the brain arrives at because of previous experience, the automatic reaction to the events at hand based on those previous experiences and the events occurring at the moment—all of it is experienced as if it is happening seamlessly at once, in a unified reality. We experience our personal reality within the walls of this cocoon, with no awareness or availability to gain other information.

Valery is the daughter of second generation Mexican-Americans. Up to the age of five, her parents spoke only in English to her. They only used Spanish behind closed doors while they were fighting so the girl could not understand what they were talking about. When they decided that it was time for her to learn Spanish they could not figure out why the girl cried when they tried to teach her the language.

It is pretty straightforward why the girl cried. However, most of the events that make us recoil, hideout and distort our reality are buried under layers and layers and more layers of narratives with great emotional value.

Experiencing the events with the least possible amount of information provided by the *Identity* will have us experience a delay between the thoughts provided by the brain, all the narratives, stories, and the experience of the events that are taking place at the moment. We will experience our experiences, and not the thoughts and beliefs about our experiences.

Thinking in Images rather than thinking in language will help us to develop a complex system on the right hemisphere that will make our right brain the "go to system," where we will experience life in the present moment, and our real essence, our Being. We have a great investment in our *Identity* since we experience the *Identity* as "me." Separating ourselves from the *Identity* will be experienced as our own death, and the brain will do anything to keep the integrity of this *me*. We know this from how willing we are to cut off relationships, or become physically or verbally violent when we experience and believe that our *Identity* is being attacked.

About 20 years ago, I attended an experiential workshop, which was about becoming self-empowered and learning how to empower others. There was a particular exercise that for some reason felt very challenging for me. My goal was "only" to come into acceptance of the fact that my thinking could be challenged. As willing as I was to go through the process, I could not understand the request of the trainer. I was dumbfounded; I just could not come to grips with what was requested of me. I became disoriented and sheepish, and I felt like I came to a dead end facing a white wall. Everyone was following directions and it seemed that only I was resistant. The facilitator got close to me and whispered in my ear, "What is so f*&%ing important about you?" It didn't make any sense what he told me, I felt as if I was doing something wrong.

Whether his intention was to challenge my thinking or my attachment to my thoughts, I didn't know. What I did experience for a month starting that day was a persistent headache.

All my life had been lived within the security of my own thoughts. I thought life was my thoughts and all of it was what I believed to be "me", or my ego, as I understood it then. That day was a day of grave danger, and whether that was the intention of the exercise or not, the demand as I interpreted it was to break away from whom I believed I was. I needed to sacrifice my *Identity*. So rather than experience that death my mind shut down, it claimed ignorance and cut all flow of information that was not consistent with the "me" of the *Identity*.

The left hemisphere with its language center and being home for the *Identity* is all about the past; and in this case, the emotional past and future. The left brain is all about sequencing information/events and protection, narrowing our attention and excluding everything that doesn't pertain to this linear arrangement.

The experiences that have more information attached to them are the ones that brand us emotionally. Experiencing the world from the right brain, "Being," is about connection and the whole, not differences but similarities.

When I lost my left hemisphere and its language centers, I also lost the clock that would break my moments into consecutive brief instances. Instead of having my moments prematurely stunted, they became open-ended, and I felt no rush to do anything. Like Walking along the beach, or just hanging out in the beauty of nature, I shifted from the doing-consciousness of my left brain to the being-consciousness of my right brain. I morphed from feeling small and isolated to feeling enormous and expansive. I stopped thinking in language and shifted to taking new pictures of what was going on in the present moment. I was not capable of deliberating about past or future-related ideas because those cells were incapacitated. All I could perceive was right here, right now, and it was beautiful...

... Although the ego center of our language center prefers defining our self as individual and solid, most of us are aware that we are made up of trillions of cells, gallons of water, and ultimately everything about us exists in a constant and dynamic state of activity. My left hemisphere had been trained to perceive myself as a solid, separate from others. Now, released from that restrictive circuitry, my right hemisphere relished in its attachment to the eternal flow, I was no longer isolated and alone. My soul was as big as the universe and frolicked with glee in a boundless sea.

MY STROKE OF INSIGHT, A BRAIN SCIENTIST'S
PERSONAL JOURNEY
BY JILL BOLTE TAYLOR, PH.D. 2008

EIGHT: The Fundamentals of Thinking in Images; of Being

I decided that it was not wisdom that enabled [poets] to write their poetry, but a kind of instinct or inspiration, such as you find in seers and prophets who deliver all their sublime messages without knowing in the least what they mean.

SOCRATES APOLOGY
BY PLATO, 399 BCE

Shedding light on what has at some point been dark gives us the opportunity for choice.

We are all born with a fundamental essence. It gives us the experience of belonging. It allows us to experience the world as connected and we flow with its experience. It is nurtured by physical contact and demonstrations of care.

This essence very early in our lives starts to get buried as we start collecting the information that will make up our *Identity*. With time, we start detaching from this essence and seldom do we experience it again. Protection becomes our main concern, thus giving us a world experience of danger; *Identity* becomes our stronghold where we experience ourselves as separate. When the concept of "I" is formed, we experience separateness.

Ultimately, our brain takes over this structure—the *Identity*, and becomes its voice. The chattering voice, the narrator of life, is the one we confide in, to interpret our emotions and keep us protected. Since this is happening between our ears, we believe that it is ourselves generating every thought, and that the voice we hear is our voice.

However, once we realize the brain is acting on its own and the majority of the thoughts we experience are thoughts generated by the brain-*Identity*, the door is open for us to escape that reality and enter the present moment where we can experience life as it is happening, experience relationships intimately, and make decisions that are in agreement with our essence and not our need of protection.

This essence, this true nature is not an intellectual creation, it doesn't need protection, it *just is*. Its qualities are belonging and compassion (sympathetic consciousness of others' distress together with a desire to alleviate it). When the *Identity* stops being the only reality available, we step into this essence, into Being that is belonging, where I am part of others, and my needs are fulfilled when other's needs are fulfilled.

The "I", or more plainly the "*Identity*" is a function of the mind. The "I" organizes and interprets external stimulus, assesses and categorizes reality. In its defensive function, it creates the illusion of separateness.

Interestingly, we are at odds with our very own nature. We are social beings. We are in relationships and we fight constantly for individuality, as if there is no "me" if I belong. We can't possibly achieve our full potential by being apart, the same way an atom of iron cannot hold a building, and a letter cannot be a novel.

At an early age, we start to be molded into the structure that is already laid out for us —the one that we get to conform to. That is, the world, society and the rules that govern your particular culture in which you were born.   The freedom that you experienced when you were a small kid and everyone was your friend, starts to disappear and the world as you knew it starts to become fragmented, cornering you and isolating you. In most of the world, *Identity* and uniqueness are not only encouraged but demanded. The underlying message is that you must be distinct. In distinction, there is "me" and there is "you." The "me" gets to be defined and so does the "you."

The sense of separation and fear consumes a great deal of the energy and the resources that could be used for creation or enjoyment. As a separate entity, from this point on, the fight is for self-preservation; to preserve the idea I have of "me." Wars and deterioration of relationships take place on this ground. My sole purpose becomes to validate whom I think I am, and the "other," with its needs, becomes the enemy and an encroachment on my very existence. As if there is not enough for both of us. And we believe that there isn't.

We become ignorant that a safe world is one of belonging. In belonging the focus is not "me", in belonging it is "we."

George grew up in Los Angeles knowing that he would be stopped by the police at any moment, and then he was. He is an educated kid raised by his mom, a University professor and author. George is black (African-American), and he is acquainted with views from both white and black people about standing out for the way he looks. Growing up, he heard his uncle from the South ranting about race about how he sees all white people as racists, and how resentful he is about the way blacks are treated. George is a well-groomed man and has a few university degrees, but he is still cautious because people treat him differently. His experience is that people are on guard before they get to know him, and he probably is too.

He was elected to a public position in the City of Los Angeles. A little after his election, he was stopped by a police. After he showed him his credentials, the policeman was courteous and helpful.

Later, George shared, "This is what it must feel like to be white."

We become the enforcers of societal beliefs, and once we incorporate those beliefs and make them "me", we don't question them. We seek only to validate them.

Once a belief sinks in and becomes part of our *Identity*, we don't question it. We defend it, justify it, and if intellectually we can't make it prevail, we attack the integrity of the individual verbally or physically so the end picture fits our belief.

Belonging is not depending on the "other." Most of the time we choose not to belong because the possibility of abandonment is too scary as it is the possibility of pain that may come with our attention being unreciprocated.

When we experience life away from and outside of our *Identity*, enlightenment, bliss, happiness is manifested, we experience something bigger within ourselves. When we are empowered by freedom from the *Identity*, the result is belonging.

Experiencing joy and happiness, and connected with something more meaningful than the needs of the *Identity* is what we all want. What we want is to belong, to be a part of something. What we want is to have access to all our resources and all our knowledge, and to have the best life experience possible.

This has been at the heart of every philosopher, and it is the objective of most practices and beliefs. It is the cornerstone of all of them.

In order for us to accomplish this, to live in a world in which people as a whole are willing to pursue these shared goals and achieve a shared reality that is immensely bigger than the reality of the *Identity*; a world in which we can combine efforts to advance each other's lives in every aspect, we have to uncover and recover the essence that we were born with that somehow we have buried and traded for protection, in our pursuit of individuality and the *Identity* that feeds it.

NINE: Consciousness, our Ability to be Aware of Self and to Witness our Actions, to be an Observer

I suppose it is tempting, if the only tool you have is a hammer, to treat everything as if it were a nail.

TOWARD A PSYCHOLOGY OF BEING
BY ABRAHAM MASLOW, 1962

We have become the story, the movie playing in our heads.

We all want to experience happiness and contentment. We want these experiences to be a permanent part of our lives, but before we can achieve that we must feel safe, feel that we belong and that we matter. Without these three essential elements, a person cannot perform, innovate, feel emotionally engaged, or move forward.

A sense of safety, belonging, and mattering are essential for us to be able to step out of the world of the *Identity*, and to be able to perform efficiently at work, at home, and in life overall. We need to experience a greater feeling of safety, both emotional and physical, so that we can take risks. The greater the feeling of connection with others, or the feeling that we're in this together and belong together, the greater the feeling that we personally matter and are contributing to the greater good. This means greater success for the company, the relationship, the family, the team, and the individual.

In every communication, every interaction, and every conflict, either we are subconsciously reinforcing the beliefs of the *Identity*, or we are experiencing safety, belonging and mattering or a combination of these.

Neurosis: Distorted perception of reality. The difficulty the individual has in sorting out information that has great emotional value for her.

Neurotic: The individual that has challenges sorting out information.

Neurotic claim: The need for protection and the need for balance.

The inner dictates, exactly like political tyranny in a police state, operate with a supreme disregard for the personas own psychic condition-for what he can feel or do as he is at present. One of the frequent shoulds, for instance, is that one should never feel hurt. As an absolute (which is implied in the "never") anyone would find this extremely hard to achieve. How many people have been, or are, so secure in themselves, so serene, as never to feel hurt? ...But the person who feels that he should never feel hurt does not have so concrete a program in mind. He simply issues an absolute order to himself, denying or overriding the fact of his existing vulnerability.

NEUROSIS AND HUMAN GROWTH: THE STRUGGLE TOWARD SELF-REALIZATION BY KAREN HORNEY, 1950

Our brain is constantly accessing the information of the *Identity* and is on the lookout for any danger that could challenge or jeopardize the integrity of the *Identity*, and we are not aware of this. For the *Identity*, depending on the individual, there is always a possibility or certainty of danger in every interaction. In relationships, the satisfaction of safety is demanded from the other person, and we can be very aggressive in our pursuit of it.

Our brain is in charge of our physical wellbeing and will spring into action, sending out all the necessary commands to keep us safe. We have called these actions reflexes, or actions that happen before we are consciously engaged. This is the brain in action, acting on its own to protect the integrity of our physical being.

When the brain determines that our *Identity* is in jeopardy, it will send us physical signals to prompt us into action. For those whose *Identity* is very defined, any perceived attack on it will be faced with retaliation or retreat. Any action is deemed fair by the individual as long as his "integrity" is kept intact. The brain cannot distinguish real physical danger from non-life-threatening emotional danger, which is why we are willing to go to extremes to avoid fear, pain or the possibility of pain.

A well-known American science writer and a well-known spiritual guide that has brought a great insight to many were having a televised debate that I was very excited about. On one side was the skeptical, no-nonsense scientist and on the other was the spiritual guru. What could possibly result from this combination? What new ideas could come out of this meeting of the minds and souls? What could be created that is different from what we already knew? I was excited and so was my family.

The room at Caltech was full of authors, scientists, intellectuals, students and regular folks who were here to somehow become transformed by new ideas. Why else would all of us take the time to be here anyway?

It took very little time after the introductions and the first question for this meeting of the minds to become a war between Identities. The answers were directed to undermine the other. By their expressions and actions, we could conclude that this exchange was personal. As brilliant as these two men are, they could not simply access their knowledge and wisdom, and the meeting became a name-calling affair, schoolyard fight. Despite all the knowledge these two have, there was no collaboration. There was no sense of wonder. Ideas flew out of the auditorium and we were left with two people using their minds as a weapon, looking for personal victory.

I still have a great respect for both of them and yet what I have witnessed was two men immersed in the world of the *Identity*, losing contact with reality. It is more common that we think and it happens to all of us, yet we don't need to be defined by it.

Their focus was on their differences and not their similarities; one is positioning while the other is discovering.

There is nothing we can do to change this subconscious programming as much as we may try, because the information is already recorded and stored. The information that makes up that program is what the brain accesses to evaluate our experiences as they happen. In other words, the brain is trying to predict what our experiences will be in the future in order to limit uncertainty. When no other reality is available, we experience life with this limited information and consistently forecast pain with the ever-present feeling of fear.

The root of all is all the information, learned values and shared truths that get stored in our brain via neuropaths, and our primal reactions when we experience a threat to those beliefs we consider to be "me."

Creating a delay on our emotional being will allow us to experience life away from the *Identity* and from its information, giving us the opportunity to experience a reality away from our thoughts.

Imagine a tent in the middle of a forest. This forest is bountiful with everything in it that is beautiful and useful. The forest is life. The tent is your *Identity*. In the tent are all our past memories and all the information we have accumulated throughout the years. The movies in our memories are constantly being projected on the walls of this tent. We don't experience these movies as movies, but as reality. The noise outside the tent we hear is muffled and intermittently interrupted by the voices inside the tent, the voices of the movies.

Inside the tent, everything is predictable. The tent is the whole universe for us when we are inside, and there is no other reality. We stay inside this tent to shield ourselves from fear and pain. Outside the tent is uncertainty and fear of the possibility of pain, but being human comes with these two innate emotions. Embracing them will allow us to walk out of the tent and experience a Universe outside the universe of our mind and our *Identity*. The information in the tent won't change and you will still listen to the movies once you are out, but the tent won't be the only reality for you.

Research and work presented at the beginning of the 20th century brought ideas to the general public that challenged general established beliefs that view the individual as powerless against the voices in his/her head, and where the voices were devils or spirits that took over a person. It took a lot of work and information to turn the power back to the individual and popularize the role of the expert who was the bridge between the individual and his thoughts. All this work created a significant shift in the world as to how we relate to our emotional conflicts.   What this campaign did was create a different relationship with the stuff that happened in between our ears, and it was of a great importance, because with the new information, individuals that were not functional and marginalized were able to join the society, their illnesses were not stigmatized, and now they were accepted.

We find now with all the distractions and the need to belong to a specific group that we are more challenged than ever, and that we experience more dissatisfaction now than we have in the last century. We are more detached from people and from our relationships than ever before. There are more demands placed on what makes us feel good right here, right now and less time expended in discovering or relating. Society is more fragmented now than before because of how easy it is now to move. The neighborhoods change fast, not allowing us the opportunity to create long-term relationships and solid communities. All this brings uncertainty to our lives and the need to find a way to ease the emotional burden of fear of the unknown and the pain of separation. Relationships become shallow and the emphasis is on our immediate needs.

Every human being has both sets of forces within him. One set clings to safety and defensiveness out of fear, tending to regress backward, hanging onto the past, afraid to grow away from the primitive communication with the mother's uterus and breast, afraid to take chances, afraid to jeopardize what he already has, afraid of independence, freedom and separateness. The other set of forces impels him forward to wholeness of Self and uniqueness of Self, toward full functioning of all his capacities, toward confidence in the face of the external world at the same time that he can accept his deepest, real, unconscious Self.

TOWARDS A PSYCHOLOGY OF BEING
BY ABRAHAM MASLOW, 1962

TEN: Separation

I jump up: it would be much better if I could only stop thinking. Thoughts are the dullest things. Duller than flesh. They stretch out and there's no end to them and they leave a funny taste in the mouth. Then there are words, inside the thoughts, unfinished words, a sketchy sentence which constantly returns: "I have to fi. . . I ex. . . Dead . . . M. de Roll is dead . . . I am not ... I ex. . ." It goes, it goes . . . and there's no end to it. It's worse than the rest because I feel responsible and have complicity in it. For example, this sort of painful rumination: I exist, I am the one who keeps it up. I. The body lives by itself once it has begun. But though I am the one who continues it, unrolls it. I exist. How serpentine is this feeling of existing, I unwind it, slowly. ... If I could keep myself from thinking! I try, and succeed: my head seems to fill with smoke . . . and then it starts again: "Smoke . . . not to think . . . don't want to think ... I think I don't want to think. I mustn't think that I don't want to think. Because that's still a thought." Will there never be an end to it?

My thought is me: that's why I can't stop. I exist because I think . . . and I can't stop myself from thinking. At this very moment, it's frightful, if I exist, it is because I am horrified at existing. I am the one who pulls myself from the nothingness to which I aspire: the hatred, the disgust of existing, there are as many ways to make myself exist, to thrust myself into existence. Thoughts are born at the back of me, like sudden giddiness, I feel them being born behind my head ... if I yield, they're going to come round in front of me, between my eyes, and I always yield, the thought grows and grows and there it is, immense, filling me completely and renewing my existence.

NAUSEA
BY JEAN PAUL SARTRE, 1938

Without the support of language and its infinite string of narratives, stories and the emotional value we attach to them, we get closer to the events, experiencing emotions that are connected to the facts rather than fabricated emotions that are related to thoughts and beliefs we created about the facts.

Our desire has been about how to find peace, fullness in life, contentment. The freedom and the power of doing rather than reacting as if the world and life was something that was invading our space. The biggest obstacle is that we have been fighting for independence; for "me" separated from the whole. Once we declare "me" we become separated and everything else looks menacing.

It is not that we have more problems now than before or that we have become worse human beings. What I have noticed is that the relation that we have with our brain has become more complex, and we are far removed from understanding the intricacy of the processing of information the brain does. Even stating this, speaking of the brain as a foreign object still lands a little out of place. I have lived my life in an intimate relationship with my mind, my thoughts, and my brain. Notice that I say, "my." The minimum amount required for a relationship to occur is two. Then more accurate thing would be to say that there is no relationship, because my mind, my brain, my *Identity* is "me." We experience it as being one and the same. No breakage of communication, it happens all at once, I think my thoughts, I give the commands, I take the actions in my life. I am in control.

Fred has challenges in social settings. He feels threatened by physical proximity, and interprets other people bumping into him as a deliberate act of aggression. He doesn't have a way to see outside his beliefs and challenges, therefore his interpretation needs to make sense in the context of how he sees the world. He sees people as jealous and mean, and believes they don't care about him, so he takes on an aggressive role with the people around him. Consequently, people are less inclined to include him, which in exchange validates his beliefs. Throughout all this he keeps control, the world is how he sees it; everything is in its right place.

Control is very important for us, it signifies security and certainty. Not having control means, chaos, unpredictability, uncertainty, fear, and powerlessness.

To create that "security," the balance between what we believe and reality, we need to become certain that what we believe is reflected in what we are experiencing. In the process, we take information and rationalize it so that it fits our views, opinions, and beliefs.

We want people to remain the same; we break them into pieces to accommodate the idea we already have of them. We like familiarity.

Unfortunately, security doesn't mean a better life, happiness, or joy. Security means that what we believe to be true becomes true. We will do anything for these beliefs to be realized.

In one of the self-development and leadership training that I was conducting, I had a team of coaches that helped coach the students. Among these coaches were two ladies that knew each other since they were kids. They went to school together and backpacked through Europe together. Another of the coaches, Angie, complained that these two were excluding her, because every time there was a break the two of them walked out of the training room together. Although the breaks were for the coaches to do whatever they wanted, the two decided to start to include Angie every time they went out. It worked for the first few times, but after those initial times, I noticed that Angie managed to stay back missing the decision the two friends were making regarding where to go. Angie managed to be left behind.

Angie's early life was marked by a lot of fighting between her parents, and she was neglected often and physically punished.

A person who believes people always take advantage and disrespect him/her will be on the lookout for these kinds of actions from others. They may interpret a smile as a smirk. A person who forgets a request will be seen as disrespectful. They may go to such extremes as to think that the other person believes herself to be better than him.

Information is constantly being gathered and our beliefs are being reinforced and enriched. All this happens over time. Often my clients declare with bewilderment that when they were younger, they felt more free spirited, more social, and less angry. The reason is that the layers of information reinforcing those emerging beliefs are more complex now than they were before. This is the consequence of years of interactions that validated those beliefs.

Beliefs are just information that we happen to attach emotional value to.

The color black is considered the color of mourning in Western and Mediterranean countries; however, it is considered a color of modesty in some Muslim cultures. The color white in Japan is generally the color of mourning the death.

These emotional values can have a great impact on the way we feel, experience and relate in life if they are not questioned.

If you are given a red rose, you may interpret this as a romantic gesture, and it may make you feel happy and hopeful about the possibilities of that relationship. It will raise your temperature and release certain chemicals that may make you experience excitement. So the reaction is physical. If instead of a red rose you received a yellow rose from someone that you were romantically interested in, this gesture may make you feel disenchanted or offended because for you, a yellow rose may signify friendship and not romance. You may feel less than, unimportant and also release some chemicals that will contribute to a state of sadness.

Although a rose is just a rose, we somehow participate in shared realities that give the color of a rose a meaning that is backed up by an emotion that we learn with time to experience and reinforce. That is all. We have created many of these categories with an emotional value attached to them. We may interpret someone not standing to say hello as an insult and retaliate as a result.

We may make things really complicated for us because we like to think of ourselves as very complex. We lose clarity in all the categories of emotions we have created, and the emotional value we placed on things, ideas, social customs, and the expectations we have in others overrides reality.

We definitely don't want things to be this simple. We are humans, and we want to think of ourselves complex and unique. I think we are less complex than we experience ourselves to be. We guard our *Identity* as if our lives depended on it, and because of this, we can't experience life.

This is why people experience that as they get older they run out of options. The information we have been accumulating through the years makes us more detached from reality, making it more difficult to perform or advance in our careers and our relationships, and we may become cynical.

I am from Colombia. In that country, at least when I lived there 30 plus years ago, we didn't insult each other with the middle finger as it is done here in the States. So when I started driving in Los Angeles, I drove like a Colombian, swerving in and out of lanes. My driving irritated other drivers, and I got the finger a lot. I didn't have any value for that sign. I didn't know what it meant. It was funny to me seeing these faces lifting their arms with a single finger sticking out. I didn't know what to make of it. I could tell that they were upset, but the single middle finger didn't mean anything to me. Come on, only one finger? Soon enough, I started jokingly lifting my arm, mimicking their attitude with five fingers up in the air and then smiling about the silliness of the whole thing. Five fingers definitely outdo their one. It was fun, for a while. Some people actually got a laugh from the whole exchange and we both drove away smiling, often they were not as angry. The fun ended when I incorporated and shared the value of the middle finger. Then it went from fun to an actual feeling— the feeling of being insulted. Now my temperature rose and not out of excitement. I even almost crashed into someone to teach him a lesson for "insulting" me.

The consolidation of our beliefs and our reality as we experience it is a complex and interesting process. It takes a consistent flow of information that is glued together by what we at some point concluded to be true. The longer I was exposed to the finger gesture and the expression of anger from the drivers, the thought that the gesture was directed to hurt me, insult me, and attack me started to occur. After this point there was no hope for freedom for me anymore, *the finger had me.*

The finger is just a simple example of how we can trace how we came to believe what we believe.

Remember Francis from Chapter TWO, that she used to clean until her fingers bled? She had a challenging childhood with an abusive father and a weak mom. Although her father called her "my princess" and was very caring with her, she didn't feel comfortable with him. The chaos the house was when he came home was overwhelming for the small girl. Her father was very abusive towards her mom. She could not stand this behavior, and it created such an emotional chaos upon seeing her father behave this way and her mom become disempowered, that one day she picked up a knife and confronted her dad. As valiant as her actions were, she was deeply hurt. This was not the relationship she wanted with her dad.

Kids usually question themselves, subconsciously. They think, "What is wrong with me? Why can't I have a normal family?" and many times resent themselves for having the thoughts they have towards either parent. Their parents are their universe; anything that alters that universe will have a great impact on how the child sees the world and themselves.

Francis' relations were marked by a feeling that she was a stranger, that she was undeserving of her girlfriend and the relationship. When she demanded attention it was in an accusatory way,

"You don't value my opinions, you are not proud of me." All her communications came from her own belief that she was not complete, that something in her was missing. Shortly after a relationship began, she would start the process of disengagement.

The consolidation of our beliefs is a complex and interesting process. It starts with us having expectations about how things should be or shouldn't be. The fact that in our private thoughts we are capable to fulfill what we want and that things are obtainable does not reflect in our "real" life.

As we run into obstacles—abusive parents, siblings, family dynamics that don't encourage compassion, stressful environments at home or at school, we start to gather information and begin to believe that what we want is an illusion, and that reality is what we have concluded about our experiences. The longer we have been gathering information about how the world is, the more susceptible we are to being upset by any change our dreamed plan encounters in real time. What this means is that throughout time, we have gathered enough information to *know* that things will always be the same, and that we *know* it from experience.

We have plenty of evidence: failed relationships, failed careers, failed businesses, etc. We start to react, and we are in permanent alert mode as if the world and everything in it is unsafe. Relationships, careers, and dreams become unobtainable, so we stop trying.

As children, we are especially sensitive to this repeated stress activation because our brains and bodies are just developing; high doses of adversity affect brain structure and function. Something that at some point was entertaining and harmless can become hurtful, dangerous, and emotionally tasking.

The middle finger gesture didn't change me. I am the same person I was before. The layers of information about this middle finger that contributed to what it became for me, is quite rich. The continuous exposure to information we have accumulated about people, insults, painful events in our lives, and rejection is what created the value system that we now give to that once emotionally harmless gesture.

We do the same with people around us. We morph them into what we want and then we go on to validate our creation. Since we act out of an aversion to fear we limit the other person's actions so they perform the expected role that will validate our perception of them.

Have you ever tried to be right at another person's expense, or at the cost of the relationship, or have you been made to feel wrong? That is our *Identity* dictating our actions. We experience not being right as losing. And losing is a complex experience, often equating to embarrassment, losing face, looking bad, losing respect, being taken advantage of, feeling less than, feeling useless, hurt, attacked, and so on. The emotional value that we give to these and the consequent physical feelings we experience are unavoidable; how can it not be real?

If we have been exposed to emotional abuse, physical abuse, sexual abuse, emotional or physical neglect, or if we have witnessed our mothers being treated violently, witnessed our fathers physically or verbally abused or diminished, if we grew up with someone in the household using alcohol and/or drugs, grew up with a mentally-ill person in the household, lost a parent due to separation or divorce, grew up with a household member in jail or prison, this exposure to early adversity affects the developing brain and bodies of children in such areas as the pleasure and reward center of the brain, which is implicated in substance dependence. It inhibits parts of the brain that are necessary for impulse control and executive function, critical areas for learning. In MRI scans we see measurable differences in the amygdala, the brain's fear response center. So there are real neurological reasons why folks exposed to high doses of adversity are more likely to engage in high-risk behavior, all having to do with the brain and body's stress response system, that governs our fight or flight response. We do anything to distract us from experiencing emotional chaos.

All this comes together to create a tight-knit reality that we can't escape. Once we record it, it is always there, ready and available to "help" us interpret reality.

Our brain, with the "Intel" at hand collected by the *Identity*, devotes itself to our emotional protection. It sees a threat at every corner and an attacker at every turn. The world becomes what the *Identity* believes it to be. The world and everything in it is experienced to be unsafe. Feelings of disengagement appears, like depression, to cope with a world in which I am powerless.

Peter B from Chapter SEVEN is an accomplished scientist who works for a big company. His leadership abilities have his fellow scientists who are levels above him seeking his guidance. His father was a product of a family that didn't pay much attention to their kids and was very lacking in the nurturing department. His mom grew up in a very aggressive and competitive environment in which there was very little appropriateness in terms of emotional display.

Part of his story includes the fact that as a little kid his younger sister suffered episodes of epilepsy. His parents were very involved in the care of his little sister who often had to be taken to the hospital at a moment's notice. There wasn't a plan to take care of his emotional wellbeing, so he experienced being left out of the family circle and cast out. This went on for a few years, and after his sister passed on, her parents were so involved with their pain and the desire to replace their little girl that he was not provided with the emotional care he needed. When he tried to join his mother in crying as she was mourning the death of his sister, his mom corrected him for her own reasons. She was alarmed that Peter was also crying, and eventually he felt too inadequate to express his emotions. He started to question if there was something wrong with him. How was he supposed to feel?

These experiences had him caught up between his love for his mom, his feelings of abandonment and the chaotic emotions he felt, not having an appropriate outlet to express any of these.

So the attention was brought inward, and self-loathing thoughts appeared. "Something must be wrong with me since nobody cares," was his underlying belief. He took refuge in fantasy books and videogames, isolating himself in a cocoon in which he had control.

Fast forwarding, at his new job as a part of a big corporation, he waited until the last minute to turn in reports. "Nobody cares anyway, let's wait until someone comes and, pushes me to do it." That was what he profoundly believed. It is easier to watch Netflix and isolate himself than confront a world that he doesn't have control of.

He didn't feel he had any value. His diplomas, abilities and the great reviews his peers gave him didn't make up any part of his reality. His reality consisted of feeling like he didn't have control and had nothing valuable to contribute. He viewed his performance as sub-par.

In addition to this, he had failed relationships that supported his desire to hurt his parents by not giving them the daughter they wanted and his distrust of women.

The longer we have been gathering information about how the world is, the more susceptible we are to any changes we encounter in real time. We start reacting more frequently, and we are in permanent alert mode as if the world and everything in it is unsafe. On one hand, we have a possible resolution in which we view ourselves as being at peace, and others accept our ideas or actions and we accept theirs. The result that we want to achieve is one where everyone is content. We really want inclusiveness. This is our ideal outcome, and the one we dream of.

However, what leads us are not those goals, but self-preservation. We get scared and we narrow our attention to what is presenting a threat to us, and we try to get hold of what gives us security. The idea of a peaceful outcome in which everyone is content disappears and we are now single mindedly pursuing control, we start to exclude.

Joe, the Marine from Chapter ONE, grew up in an emotionally chaotic family. That was his experience. This environment was scary and unsafe, and he felt that he was not being cared for. Being the only male, and despite being the youngest, he took it upon himself to fix things in the family and tried to be a good boy. This gave him a sense of control and emotional fulfillment in this otherwise emotionally chaotic environment.

Being a leader at home and at school on the football team gave him enough emotional connections without the risk of emotional uncertainty. As a Marine Sergeant, he cared deeply for his men. He didn't lose any of them in the invasion of 2003, and things developed on his command. Again he was in control, by caring for people and fixing things he stayed connected without the emotional danger and uncertainty of someone taking care of him.

His girlfriend Laura experienced abandonment all her life and had physically as well as verbally abusive relationships. She had been made to feel wrong often and as a consequence of the abandonment, she believes there is something wrong with her.

In Joe and Laura's relationship, Laura is all about validation and Joe about fixing things. She believes that people will hurt her or abandon her and she believes that there is something wrong with her. Joe wants emotional protection and the safety that control can give him.

Here is a situation encountered by Joe and Laura, and how they experience it given their own specific needs in the relationship and their need for self-preservation.

This is Joe's account of what went on during the exchange:

We were talking on the phone and I asked her about us spending time together on the weekend. She told me last Sunday that this Friday she was going to a friend's birthday party, and that it was a two-day trip, but she only wanted to participate on Friday... Today she said she's going to stay both days and I said, "Ok, is there any time this weekend you'd be free for us to spend some time together?" She said, "To do what?" I said, "Hike or swim... It doesn't matter. I'd just like to see you." She kept going around the subject and then I said, calmly, "If you don't want to see each other this weekend, then it's ok." She yelled and said it was mean for me to say that, then she hung up. I'm pretty confused and not sure if I should do anything or just let it go.

He said it was ok. Not saying it was ok would put him in a situation in which he has no control. Acknowledging that he wanted time with her would be admitting that he was dependent on her fulfilling or not fulfilling his emotional need. Now in her indecisiveness, he feels unable to determine the outcome of the situation, and there is a possibility that his demands may not be met immediately.

Now, he gets back in control by saying "It is ok", and not disclosing his needs.

His "confusion" arises from his attachment to the outcome. That is how he intellectualizes and experiences a situation he doesn't have control of. He can't admit and accept the pain of separation he is experiencing, so instead he claims confusion.

For Lisa, Joe's reassurance is interpreted as him not caring and her being left alone, abandoned; so she shut down to protect herself.

The way control looks like is we are right and they are wrong, that they are trying to hurt us and we have the evidence of it. Well, we are willing to make everyone wrong, even if they are not, so we go over the conversations or the facts as we remember them and every time we find more evidence that we are right, and we go through this process over and over. The more we do it the more removed we are from reality and from our original goal. Finally, we may realize that we choose the "wrong" people to be with, or the "wrong" career, and when we move into the next relationship or career often we discover that our experience is the same as in the previous one.

Neurosis: Distorted perception of reality. The difficulty the individual has in sorting out information that has great emotional value for her/him.

Neurotic: The individual that has challenges sorting out information.

Neurotic claim: The need for protection and the need for emotional balance and the strategy to achieve it.

"As always happens in neurosis, needs turn into claims, which means that he feels entitled to having all these goods come to him. The needs for love, affection, understanding, sympathy, or help turn into: I am entitled to love, affection, understanding, empathy. I am entitled to have things done for me. I am entitled not to the pursuit of happiness but to have happiness fall into my lap. It goes almost without saying that these claims --as claims-remain more unconscious than in the expansive type.

The relevant questions in this regard are: upon what does the self-effacing type base his claims and how does he assert them? The most conscious, and in a way realistic, basis is that of his endeavors to make himself agreeable and useful. Varying with his temperament, his neurotic structure, and the situation, he may be charming, compliant, considerate, sensitive to the wishes of others, available, helpful, sacrificing, understanding. It is but natural that he overrates what, in this or that way, he does for another person. He is oblivious to the fact that the latter may not at all like this kind of attention or generosity; he is unaware that there are strings attached to his offers; he omits from his consideration all the unpleasant traits he has. And so it all appears to him as the pure gold of friendliness, for which he could reasonably expect returns.

Another basis for his claims is more detrimental for himself and more coercive of others. Because he is afraid to be alone, others should stay at home; because he cannot stand noise, everybody should tiptoe around the house. A premium is thus set on neurotic needs and suffering. Suffering is unconsciously put into the service of asserting claims, which not only checks the incentive to overcome it, but also leads to inadvertent exaggerations of suffering. This does not mean that his suffering is merely put on for demonstrative purposes. It affects him in a much deeper way because he must primarily prove to himself, to his own satisfaction, that he is entitled to the fulfillment of his needs. He must feel that his suffering is so exceptional and so excessive that it entitles him to help. In other words this process makes a person actually feel his suffering more intensely than he would without its having acquired an unconscious strategic value."

NEUROSIS AND HUMAN GROWTH: THE
STRUGGLE TOWARD SELF-REALIZATION
BY KAREN HORNEY, 1950

ELEVEN: Experience Before Reference

Severe punishment unquestionably has an immediate effect in reducing a tendency to act in a given way. This result is no doubt responsible for its widespread use. We 'instinctively' attack anyone whose behavior displeases us—perhaps not in physical assault, but with criticism, disapproval, blame, or ridicule. Whether or not there is an inherited tendency to do this, the immediate effect of the practice is reinforcing enough to explain its currency. In the long run, however, punishment does not actually eliminate behavior from a repertoire, and its temporary achievement is obtained at tremendous cost in reducing the overall efficiency and happiness of the individuals.

SCIENCE AND HUMAN BEHAVIOR
BY B.F. SKINNER, 1951

For a flying bird, understanding the physics of its flight and the mechanics of its movement in the air does not matter. What it does is fulfilling its nature, so it flies. We, like the bird, want to fulfill our true nature.

We start as "experiencers," present to life's events. However, as we start to identify ourselves with the events in our life, we start to lose all the available possibilities the experiencer has, and we become entangled with the needs that arise from the *Identity* and all its information, and the intellectualization that makes sense of what is being experienced. This system dictates our course of action and determines what is real and what is not. This system creates a sense of certainty and contains no possibilities, fulfills our needs for emotional security, our need to have and to control. It erases the present from our view, and begin to relate with satisfying our need to "know" and "have." Fear of detachment and of separation, and focusing on only one possibility, makes all other possibilities disappear.

Possibilities are alternative routes, resources to get our wants fulfilled but are unfamiliar. The *Identity* is what is familiar; it is what makes me, "me."

Most of us want the feeling of peace and security. We want the power that comes with having no need for protection, however, the obstacle we face is the fear and the pain of letting go of "me/*Identity*" what I believe to be true, the true me.

The particulars of the unfavorable environmental conditions are different in each case, as are those of the course the development takes, and its outcome. But it always impairs the inner strength and coherence of the individual, and thereby always generates certain vital needs for remedying the resulting deficiencies. Although these are closely interwoven, we can distinguish the following aspects:

Despite his early attempts at solving his conflicts with others, the individual is still divided and needs a firmer and more comprehensive integration.

For many reasons, he has not had the chance to develop real self-confidence: his inner strength has been sapped by having to be on the defensive, by his being divided, by the way in which his early "solution" initiated a one-sided development, thereby making large areas of his personality unavailable for constructive uses. Hence, he desperately needs self-confidence, or a substitute for it.

He does not feel weakened in a vacuum, but feels specifically less substantial, less well equipped for life than others. If he had a sense of belonging, his feeling inferior to others would not be so serious a handicap. But living in a competitive society, and feeling at the bottom--as he does--isolated and hostile, he can only develop an urgent need 'to lift himself above others.'

Even more basic than these factors is his beginning alienation from self. Not only is his real self prevented from a straight growth, but in addition his need to evolve artificial, strategic ways to cope with others has forced him to override his genuine feelings, wishes, and thoughts. To the extent that safety has become paramount, his innermost feelings and thoughts have receded in importance--in fact, have had to be silenced and have become indistinct. (It does not matter what he feels, if only he is safe.) His feelings and wishes thus cease to be determining factors; he is no longer, so to speak, the driver, but is driven. Also, the division in himself not only weakens him in general, but reinforces the alienation by adding an element of confusion; he no longer knows where he stands, or "who" he is.

NEUROSIS AND HUMAN GROWTH: THE STRUGGLE TOWARD SELF-REALIZATION BY KAREN HORNEY, 1950

We already have accumulated enough information to rationalize everything in our lives, including what we feel, do and think, what others think or don't think, and everything we come in contact with.

We want to put a pause on this torrent of knowledge at least long enough to be able to experience something other than our thoughts and opinions.

We have been wanting to experience life, to see it in its true colors; this is what *Thinking in Images* is all about.

In general terms, we think in a linear way with the left side of our brain. We construct reality with a series of narratives that string together our thoughts and opinions to give some cohesive meaning to what we experience as reality. What this means is that we take an event and we build around it meanings, reasons, opinions, our intentions, other's intentions, impact, pain, fear and every imaginable element that can be attached to it in order to make sense out the event or predict a future outcome. The more impactful or repetitive the event was, the more narratives, stories and meanings we will build around them, thinking things such like, "People don't care, there is something wrong with me, I always…"

Pat shared a story that she thinks is cute about her grandson: "My daughter plays with him and tells him, 'what's wrong with you?' Now my grandson goes after his mom and in this cute whining voice asks her, 'What's wrong with me mommy?' He talks so clearly now. Isn't he cute?

Probably you too have told someone in a playful way, "What's wrong with you?" Pat's daughter uses this expression playfully to talk to her little boy who is pretty active. Now that he is 2 and a half and talking, he is starting to incorporate, "What's wrong with me?" into his world. The process will consolidate as part of who he is by adding elements to it in order to make sense of the statement, unless the process is interrupted. Anything that he may find rejection in, and he probably will find a lot of rejection being an energetic kid, will fall in the basket of, "What's wrong with me?" He already "knows" there is something wrong with him, what is missing is the content.

We have been wanting for most of our lives to be fully engaged with the things that matter to us, and to get lost in what we do, as most of us did at some point when we were kids, before the chatter in our heads started to be heard.

For most of us, this broadcasting becomes louder as time passes and we can see how this dampens our experiences and takes over every aspect of our lives. We experience life in the midst of our thoughts, leaving us empty and often with guilt, resentment and naturally, depression and anger.

We can see that life has been experienced as if it was wrapped in a cellophane paper like a delicious candy, and we found out it tasted just like the paper, as if we were licking the candy without unwrapping it. We see life through the transparent paper, we imagine the sweet taste, we have some vague memory of it, but the memory or the information we have about it does not allow us to be in contact with the real thing, or delight ourselves in the real taste.

Our right human hemisphere is all about this present moment. It's all about "right here, right now." Our right hemisphere, it thinks in pictures and it learns kinesthetically through the movement of our bodies. Information, in the form of energy, streams in simultaneously through all of our sensory systems and then it explodes into this enormous collage of what this present moment looks like, what this present moment smells like and tastes like, what it feels like and what it sounds like. I am an energy-being connected to the energy all around me through the consciousness of my right hemisphere. We are energy-beings connected to one another through the consciousness of our right hemispheres as one human family. And right here, right now, we are brothers and sisters on this planet, here to make the world a better place. And in this moment we are perfect, we are whole and we are beautiful.

My left hemisphere, our left hemisphere, is a very different place. Our left hemisphere thinks linearly and methodically. Our left hemisphere is all about the past and it's all about the future. Our left hemisphere is designed to take that enormous collage of the present moment and start picking out details, and more details about those details. It then categorizes and organizes all that information, associates it with everything in the past we've ever learned, and projects into the future all of our possibilities. And our left hemisphere thinks in language. It's that ongoing brain chatter that connects me and my internal world to my external world. It's that little voice that says to me, "Hey, you've got to remember to pick up bananas on your way home. I need them in the morning." It's that calculating intelligence that reminds me when I have to do my laundry. But perhaps most important, it's that little voice that says to me, "I am. I am."

MY STROKE OF INSIGHT, A BRAIN SCIENTIST
PERSONAL JOURNEY
BY JILL BOLTE TAYLOR, PH.D. 2008

TWELVE: What Do We Want?

Close both eyes see with the other one. Then we are no longer saddled by the burden of our persistent judgments, our ceaseless withholding, our constant exclusion. Our sphere has widened and we find ourselves quite unexpectedly in a new, expansive location in a place of endless acceptance and infinite love.

TATTOOS ON THE HEART: THE POWER OF
BOUNDLESS COMPASSION
BY GREGORY J. BOYLE, 2010

The more patient and willing you are to be comfortable with the uncomfortableness of not knowing, the more profoundly affected your view of the world and yourself will be and the more permanent the changes will be. We are throwing a monkey wrench into the machinery that has governed your world, feeding you the information that tells you your options are limited.

On and on, what my clients and the people I talk to anywhere want seems to be the same no matter the social status, educational level or ethnicity: a sense of peace, happiness, safety, a group of people around them that they can feel safe with, a significant other to share themselves with, and to impact others.

This is very apparent when I am presenting a workshop, especially the *Thinking in Images* workshop. In the safety of a workshop, people relate as they see themselves in the privacy of their own bedroom, with no titles and no social status. The only difference is that in the context of the workshop there is no place for self-judgment, people are able to truly connect authentically with themselves and others. There is no expectation from others, and there is comfort in being as they are in the moment. Because the setup is to manifest themselves as they are, there is no expectation of validation from anyone. Therefore, they have the freedom to just be.

Yes, we want to BE, just BE.

But what is to be?

To be is to experience life without the interference of our thoughts; it is us not listening to our minds while it interprets every piece of information, and resisting the temptation to believe that what the mind concludes is, at all times, reality.

The mind's main job is to protect us, and in doing so it is constantly on the lookout for danger. This leaves very little space to be connected, to be creative. The mind experiences emotional danger as a terminal and real danger, therefore the mind mobilizes all our resources for protection purposes. We experience this danger physically, your heart pounds faster, muscles tighten, blood pressure rises, breath quickens, making it very difficult to disengage from the belief that the danger is real.

When we experience life without interpretation, our experience of the world and life expands. It is now, not bound by the limited information of the mind, *Identity* that we experience a life that is richer in nuances, more abundant and less threatening. We feel connected and we are accepting of others, we draw fewer distinctions, we experience ourselves as belonging rather than separated, and we are less judgmental.

When we are part of a group we are more accepting, and we may even overlook their flaws. The opposite happens when we experience life from the confined world of the *Identity*, where there are outsiders and insiders. With people we consider to be outside of our group, we are more judgmental and quick to criticize. When we are defensive we are only in contact with our own needs. If you have ever been in a conflict with someone you know how difficult is to share common ground if you experience yourself as separated and view the other person as a threat. No matter how much we want to connect and develop intimate relationships, it becomes impossible when we are experiencing this kind of reality.

Mary had a childhood where she experienced physical, verbal and sexual abuse. Her brothers and sisters have married and moved out or immigrated to another country. At nine years old, Mary woke up to an empty house, her mom had left the country without saying a word to her.

She learned to deal with her fears by creating imaginary relationships with the people that were vendors in the streets. However, trust was not part of her beliefs. She wanted to experience the peace that trust produces, but her experiences made her believe, "The closer I get emotionally, the more in danger I am of being hurt and abandoned."

Her relationship with her husband was about doing things for him but staying away from emotional closeness. The interesting part was that she didn't see herself as distant, she felt engaged. This was affecting the dynamics of the relationship, they were stuck. He was demanding the closeness they had at the beginning of their relationship, but at this stage, she experienced the relationship with her husband as closely similar to earlier experiences of wanting to be cared for and wanting emotional connection. In her past these wants were followed by abandonment, so automatically she was protective. The way she handled disagreements was leaving him. The emotional demand was too great. She didn't want to be close enough to be rejected or abandoned. The arguments caused by the lack of closeness brought on by her insistent husband were interpreted as if there was something wrong with her, and this proved her right about the dangers of relationships.

You can imagine that experiencing a non-threatening world would in exchange have us be less defensive, therefore creating less conflict. Relationships can flourish if our attention and actions are directed towards the relationship's needs and not towards our needs as an individual and our need to *feel* safe.

But if I am not defensive, how are we going to identify a threat? Who is going to let me know, is this permission for everyone to reign free?

Many of my clients are afraid of this because they fear that another part of themselves will take over or people will take advantage of them. There is a fear that because to "be" is to shut the mind down or slow it down, that they will become unresponsive with no power to decide or guide themselves.

Up to the age of four my life was centered on love and family — mom, dad, brothers and sisters. But then it all changed. One by one, my family started to leave; some for a short time, and some permanently. My mom, a very strong woman, lived by the motto, "We don't cry, and we don't show our emotions." So I intently internalized the pain of many goodbyes. I became angry and mistrusted everyone. I believed everyone would hurt me. I did learn to draw from my love of helping others, but I was never close enough to be hurt. I never said goodbye; instead, I disappeared, leaving a lot of people angry. I knew my actions hurt people, but I couldn't do anything about it. I was unable to be intimate. I wanted to, but I was powerless. My world felt unsafe.

My dad was killed by a bus. I did not grieve. I was so numb from years of keeping people out that when I went back to my country, Colombia, I did not even ask where my father was buried.

A year later, my brother was murdered in front of his family. I did not grieve then either. I was, however, permanently angry. This feeling was safe.

In 1995, I was waiting in downtown LA to be picked up by my wife. I had just finished an intense personal development program and for the first time, at the age of 37, I was not angry. I was not in judgment. I was clean as an empty canvas. Across the street, there were several people waiting for the bus.

What I will narrate now is an afterthought. When these events happened, I was fully engaged and present, not analyzing them.

A man on the other side at the bus stop, his arms, neck, chest and part of his face covered with tattoos, was looking back in my direction. He was a gang member, and his tattoos told of his gang affiliation, incarcerations and deeds. With his eyes intently fixated on me, he started to walk in my direction. The clean canvas that I was away from my *Identity* did not register his rage. He probably thought of my blank stare as being "mad dogging" him (mad dogging in the gang world and in prison is an expressionless glare ostensibly used to intimidate – you could be hurt or even killed for it).

He left the sidewalk and walked onto the street enraged. I did not register any of this at that moment. Empty as I was, there was no place for him to project his anger. As he came closer, his expression started to change. The closer he got, the more it changed. He came as close as three inches from my face, and then he smiled and left. This man got to be in contact with something other than his anger, the dynamics at that bus stop have changed.

It dawned on me that the power and the responsibility are within me and every single human being when there is no face to be saved, when there is no "me" to be defended.

I can tell you that I am not in that space all the time. Let me correct myself, I am not in that space *most* of the time. However, that space is a moment-to-moment goal; sometimes I achieve it and sometimes I fall short, but one significant thing has changed in my life. I am not as afraid of being afraid as I once was, and many times I don't avoid pain, which makes me more compassionate with the person in front of me than I used to be. Now I am aware when I am visiting the universe of the *Identity*, so my choices are not made immediately upon that reality. It has made me more accepting of myself, and when I am in that space of acceptance everyone wins—I am less aggressive, less defensive, and less judgmental.

THIRTEEN: Why can't I get What I Want?

Properly speaking, the unconscious is the real psychic; its inner nature is just as unknown to us as the reality of the external world, and it is just as imperfectly reported to us through the data of consciousness as is the external world through the indications of our sensory organs.

THE INTERPRETATION OF DREAMS BY SIGMUND FREUD, 1899

The connections between brain cells aren't set in concrete -- they change all the time. Thus, with each new experience, your brain slightly rewires its physical structure. In fact, how you use your brain helps determine how your brain is organized. It is this flexibility, which scientists call plasticity that can help your brain rewire itself.

We are not in a relationship with what is at hand in front of us. What is available at the moment must pass an inspection. It must be scanned, because the brain is looking for anything that remotely resembles an event that was unpleasant in the past, in an attempt to prevent these events from happening again. The brain pins down all external information against the information the *Identity* has gathered while looking for similarities. We find what the mind is looking for and then we rationalize why we are "choosing" it. It is the only thing available anyway, because it is what we keep finding. And we keep finding it because it is what we have been looking for.

In the *Thinking in Images* workshops and during my sessions with clients, I give a silly example of how we spend our days and it helps them to relax and step out of their reality in order to view their lives in a different light. It goes as follows:

Imagine a beautiful meadow, the one you like. It is green, full of flowers, birds are tweeting, water is running through it, and the weather is perfect.

You are wearing your new shoes. Someone tells you to watch out so you don't step on poop, because this person has already had that experience before. Now you find yourself looking for poop and the meadow is not as crisp and clear as it was before. You are looking now for poop. There is actually not much poop considering the size of the meadow, but you don't want poop on your shoes. So you intensely look for poop, and you find poop even where there is none. Even a piece of brown bark makes you change directions.

Some of us are very surprised why there is so much poop in our lives, and what we don't realize is that we have been finding it only because we have been looking for it. Some adopt poop and think that with a little perfume it can become what we want it to be. We shrink our goals to make them consistent with what we have, and we keep spraying perfume on them because we are afraid of the pain of separation when we lose what has become familiar.

In other cases, we think we found something that's poop, and in our need for consistency, we turn it into poop.

What we really want is thrown to the back, security becomes more important than having what we truly want. The thing is that we are not aware of this. We keep making up reasons, rationalizing why things are this way. We often find the reasons outside ourselves, blaming our significant other, people's bad attitudes, and the fact that people are mean or don't understand us. Then the thought, "There may be something wrong with me," is quietly experienced.

It makes sense then that we have a difficult time navigating life, since we see and experience events and others in our life as a threat. The natural way to deal with a threat is reacting to it, attacking it, strategizing and keeping tabs on it.

To deal with fear we reduce our world to a manageable size. We stop wanting or we begin rationalizing that what we want is not as important as it once was. We demonize the people or entities that we want to have a relationship with, but we are unable to due to the great fear that stands in the way and paralyzes us or makes us clumsy. While all these are taking place we grow resentful and isolate ourselves further.

Relationships become the battleground on which we display our discontent with the life we have created and with ourselves. Although we may want the relationship, we are not relating with the person we are with, but instead with our inadequacies and our beliefs. Soon after the honeymoon has passed, we lose sight of our partner and we are on the lookout for danger.

Mark and Caroline are married. Caroline was married before and she lived a physically and verbally abusive relationship with her ex-husband. Also, when she was growing up, there were a lot of problems at home. For Mark, this is his first marriage. They both have personal issues that were affecting the relationship. She was loud and at some points she broke things in frustration. At one particularly frustrating moment for her, she came close to him and said, "Hit me."

She stopped being present to her new husband who is not abusive, fortunately for the relationship he walked away.

The Movie of our Memories

The brain seems organized around the basic processes of minimizing threat and maximizing reward. Neuroscientists have concluded that the brain networks that are used for basic survival are the same ones that ensure that we can breathe air and that we have food and water. The limbic system of the brain identifies in 1/5 of a second something that is a threat, and threats always take priority over rewards. These blindingly fast decisions occur in the limbic system and happen long before the most conscious part of the brain processes the data and reaches a conclusion.

Memories are very complex; they get stored along with all kinds of information that was related with or present at the moment the event or events took place;

including scent, taste, sound, texture, color etc. This is why a memory can be easily triggered.

When a memory is triggered, all the information regarding this memory is activated, like a complex virtual movie full of texture and holographic projections. It feels like it's the real thing. We feel, we smell, we hear; it is like we are there, we *re-live* it, we live this memory again. We shut down the outside world, only experiencing this world and it becomes real to us.

When we are experiencing the "reality" of our memory we are being hijacked from the present moment by our brain, and we are unable to relate to the outside world in real time. The outside world becomes like a faint projection, over-imposed on our new reality, like a holodeck of our own making (A holodeck is a fictional virtual reality facility featured in Star Trek). Reality here is like a distant indistinguishable voice that comes from the other side of the walls of this theater— this holodeck, where the movie of our memory is being replayed.

How many times have we been so engrossed in a memory that the world fades away, and although we have our eyes open, we don't "see" and we are not fully aware of the people around us?

FOURTEEN: Who is Thinking my Thoughts?

The conscious mind is not at the centre of the action in the brain; instead, it is far out on a distant edge, hearing but whispers of the activity.... A mere 400 years after our fall from the centre of the universe, we have experienced the fall from the centre of ourselves...There is a looming chasm between what your brain knows and what your mind is capable of accessing...

INCOGNITO: THE SECRET LIVES OF THE
BRAIN
BY DAVID EAGLEMAN, 2011

The chattering voice of the brain, the narrator of life, is the one we confide in, to interpret our emotions and keep us protected. Since this is happening between our ears, we believe that it is us generating every thought, and that the voice we hear is our voice.

A thought and the process of thinking is something that appears to be of a very ethereal nature for most of us. We seem to be able to think at will when we apply our attention to something specific; work, talking, creating, etc., but it seems there are a lot of thoughts that we can't account for. Thoughts that although we are familiar with are thoughts that have no basis in reality, but have more to do with other series of thoughts we have had before and that pop into our heads without us consciously recalling them. It feels like thoughts are something that I can't grasp or have any power over most of the time.

Understanding the nature of thoughts is essential for us to create a relationship with our brain/mind that will allow us to live in the present moment, see things for what they are, and be able to move forward using our abilities to achieve what we set out to achieve.

There is a lot of talk about being in the moment, and in the present. As Alan Watts aptly put it, "If we are talking all of the time, we never hear what anyone else has to say. In the same way, if we are talking to ourselves all the time, we are never listening; we have nothing to think about other than thoughts, and are never in relationship with reality."

We love to create stories and give them meaning. We love to hear other people's stories, and we listen to them and compare them with our own stories. The problem is that we create stories about everything in a way that is appealing to us and more often than not, they are not based on reality, especially if the thoughts are related to our emotions and/or our self-image and *Identity*.

We pride ourselves on the ability to think, "I think, therefore I am," as Descartes said. This "I" is me, I do my own thinking. It has been drilled so profoundly in our consciousness by society that it would be ludicrous to think that I don't do my own thinking at will. There is also an underlying statement that I am my thoughts.

It is quite difficult to escape this way of thinking since "society" is the one teaching us what it is to be "me." By society, I mean authors, philosophers, our friends, moms, dads and everyone we encounter and interact with, in addition to all the things we read and see.

Things become difficult and convoluted because we want to conform and be accepted into the "group." In the "group" everyone seems to be "normal," the abnormal people have been already cast out. So "I" definitely get to be "normal."

Now every thought, no matter how out of place it is, gets to be rationalized in such a way that it "fits" into my beliefs, my self-image and my idea of normalcy. This could create a much distorted picture of reality.

Psychologists believe that as many as twenty-five percent of the kids in our schools have some diagnosable disorder... statistics show that "sixty-six percent (will) never get married and have a family." Those numbers make them forget that they have power over who they become as individuals. They interpret those general statistics as a prediction for their own future, when is nothing of the sort.

More specifically, they see their future as inexorably tied to every broad, unfavorable statistic associated with their diagnosis. In that sense, some see an autism diagnosis as a sentence to some kind of death. They get swallowed up by the negative features of their diagnosis, forgetting that they've lived their lives before and that life goes on after. In short, they allow themselves to become victims of a label.

That is the danger of diagnosis. Some people read what's associate it with a label and make it self-fulfilling. They let go and become the worst of what they read. That negative outcome can be reinforced by teachers and adults who say or think, "He has a diagnosis of autism. We can't expect too much of him." That is most assuredly not the way I have lived my life.

It doesn't matter what sixty-six percent of people do in any particular situation. All that matter is what you do.

BE DIFFERENT: ADVENTURES OF A FREE-RANGE ASPERGIAN BY JOHN ELDER ROBINSON, 2011

We are living in an era where in the last 15 years we have discovered more about the mind than in the previous 2,000. Although the general public has greater access to information more than ever before, the research and findings are still in a scientific language and have not been "translated" into laymen's language; therefore a general paradigm shift has not occurred. This awareness will occur when the science behind the mind makes sense at the experiential level, becomes part of how we function at all moments and is included in every aspect of our lives, but this has not happened yet.

The biggest problem that we encounter in experiencing life as it is happening, and finding the freedom to be, is that we believe that every thought we experience is ours and that the information they carry is true.

Up to now, to believe that "my" thoughts are not mine was considered a mental illness. We have a name for it and there are medications for it and places to house these people.

The way we learn to think about our mental wellbeing or lack thereof is in terms of our symptoms. As a whole, experts and laymen have taken to explain these symptoms and how to fight them, and they have sliced the mind into pieces that are manageable, linear to our understanding, and that fits our ability to explain things. These symptoms needed to be defined so that any sensible man and woman understand them.

This way of explaining the mind's troubles has created more subdivisions of our symptoms, making it more difficult to achieve a place in which we can just "Be." Because the intellectual path is so convoluted, it is very difficult to experience a life in which we are self-generating and our environment is experienced without boundaries. It is difficult not to continue managing our resources, and instead just let it all play out.

We humans have the need to explain things. We pride ourselves in understanding things and defining them. So not being able to formulate an answer gives us a sense of confusion, and it presents a chaotic world in which we don't have a sense of control.

There is no escape from the need to explain things, that is just what the mind does. However, how can we "Be" despite this need?

This is not only a cultural way of looking at things but also a matter of pride in human beings. We want to understand and to be in control, so we center everything that makes up our understanding of the world within the confines of our physical realm. Things become "ours," including our thoughts, our ideas, our opinions, and our beliefs. Ultimately, all that becomes "me", so we walk into life being all those thoughts, and when the information at hand is inconsistent with "me", we break it into pieces to fit our information so that there is balance again.

Ben started one of our sessions complaining that his brother every time they see each other tells him, "You have changed a lot," and saying that is starting to be annoying to him.

Ben was very scared of intimate relationships. His relationships were about control, and surviving the immense stress he experienced in social settings. He didn't want to experience criticism or rejection. He also was a drinker, this helped him cope with the anxiety and fear he experienced. His relationships were tense, and although he was loved, he was also resented.

After a few sessions he developed a new relationship with fear, he embraced it and soon he was a participant in social gatherings. His relationship with his brother improved dramatically.

We have difficulty with change, whether this is because it requires a lot of adjustments in us or because we have a vested interest in keeping things as they are.

Change in others is always an encroachment on our world; it is a demand for our own change in order to be able to relate with this new person. This is why we keep referring back to what the people were, rather than what they are. As much as we want people to change, we keep poking them so that they stay the same and us remaining somehow in control.

That is why it is so important to us to be right. The smaller the world we created, the more important it is to be right. The pieces in our world are too big, and one piece alone can collapse the whole thing and send us into despair, inducing great amounts of fear that will have us locked in and unable to function. That is a feeling we don't want to experience.

We will go to any extreme to be safe. We are willing to destroy all relationships for safety's sake. How could we not? Relationships are unpredictable and can hurt a lot. Even if everything is going well, human beings have the horrible bad habit of dying.

Thoughts are just information that has been stored in our brain. They're really electro-chemical reactions — but the number and complexity of these reactions make them hard to fully understand them. There is a part of ourselves that is able to observe our thoughts as they occur and see them for what they are, but at the same time, it is difficult not to relate with these thoughts since they are happening inside of us.

Although it is just information stored in parts of our brain, when there is no alternative to this information, this becomes reality to us.

We can view this information, our thoughts, memories and beliefs, as a vivid virtual world where everything we see, hear, feel, taste and smell is an interpretation created entirely INSIDE our head. Because of this, we are seldom able to escape it, and all our actions are taken based on the information this make-believe world and my interaction with it provides.

Christine is a smart and accomplished business woman. In a meeting with a business advisor and a business partner, she experienced the advisor talking exclusively to her partner, and in the middle of the conversation, she walked away, leaving this important meeting. When questioned she said, "Obviously I am not important."

She grew up with parents who were self-involved and judgmental.

Sarah is a doctor. She is afraid of calling her employees' attention and demanding things from them. She grew up separated from her parents with authoritative brothers and sisters. She is the youngest. She wants her employees to like her.

It is the brain that "sees," and in some important ways what it sees does not reflect the information it derives from sensory input. For this reason, we are all living in our own reality simulations—abstractions that we construct as a result of both what we perceive with our senses and how our brains modify this perception.

Fear, anxiety, panic may occur as reactions both to anticipated humiliations or to ones that have taken place. Anticipatory fears may concern examinations, public performances, social gatherings, or a date; in such instances they are usually described as a "stage fright." It is a good enough descriptive term if we use it metaphorically for any irrational fear preceding public or private performance. It covers situations in which we want either to make a good impression as, for instance, on new relatives, or some important personage; or situations in which we must start new activities, such as beginning a new job, starting to paint, or going to a public speaking class. People who are afflicted with such fears often refer to them as fears of failure, disgrace, ridicule. This seems to be exactly what they are afraid of. Nevertheless, it is misleading to put it this way because it suggests a rational fear of a realistic failure. It leaves out the fact that what constitutes failure for a given person is subjective. It may encompass all that falls short of glory and perfection, and the anticipation of this possibility is precisely the essence of the milder forms of stage fright. A person is afraid of not performing as superbly as his exacting should demand, and therefore fears that his pride will be hurt. There is a more pernicious form of stage fright in it unconscious forces operate in a person, obstructing his capacities in the very act of performing. The stage fright then is a fear that through his own self-destructive tendencies he will be ridiculously awkward, forget his lines, choke up, and thus disgrace himself instead of being glorious and victorious.

Another category of anticipatory fears does not concern the quality of a person's performance but the prospect of having to do something that will hurt his special pride--such as asking for a raise or a favor, making an application, or approaching a woman--because it entails the possibility of being rejected. It may occur before sexual intercourse if the latter means for him being humiliated.

Reactions of fear also may follow insults. Many people react with trembling, shaking, perspiration, or some other expression of fear to a lack of deference or to arrogant behavior on the part of others. These reactions are a mixture of rage and fear, the fear being in part a fear of one's own violence. Similar reactions of fear may follow a feeling of shame without the latter being experienced as such. A person may suddenly feel overwhelmed by a feeling of uncertainty, or even panic, if he has been awkward, timid, or offensive.

NEUROSIS AND HUMAN GROWTH: THE STRUGGLE TOWARD SELF-REALIZATION BY KAREN HORNEY, 1950

FIFTEEN: How can I Get Something Different from what I've Gotten so Far?

I remember the first MP3 I ever downloaded. I remember the first time that I ever played a track from the internet. And I remember just thinking: you know is just information, is just audio, there's such a crazy amount of emotion, the fact that you can kind of share emotion over the internet is really wild to think that something so important to you, you can just trade so freely. So I think it's hard to quantify how important it was.

SHAWN FANNING, NAPSTER FOUNDER

Although what we believe is just information stored in parts of our brain, when there is no alternative to this information, this becomes reality to us.

We can't become different believing that the world is a world in which I can't have. Wanting to have is not the same as believing I *can* have.

Remember, our beliefs are represented in hardwired connections, and the more complex the structure, the easier it is accessed.

Since referencing, looking for information in the past and projecting it into the future is what the brain does

24/7, and because our belief is that what the brain is broadcasting is what we can conclude to be reality and nothing else, we are presented a world with no other options but the ones that are contained in the world of our thoughts. Without awareness of a world outside that one, the only options are within the confines of the "only" world we are aware of. We experience the thoughts of our mind and our own true thoughts as one seamless stream, creating the illusion of unity.

The price we pay is great because we are aware primarily of the mind's thoughts, information, and the world outside as faded superimposed images on those thoughts. This is why all women and men appear to be the same, and we zero in the similarities they have with the information the *Identity* has accumulated, rather than the differences.

Jill is a talented business woman and well known for her professionalism as well as the big projects that she has taken in the past. She was commissioned with a project for a multinational company. She encountered some resistance to her ideas and budget. With the project due date getting closer she became frustrated with negotiations.

After getting her frustrations off her chest, I asked her what the thought was that was recurring in her mind about why they were being difficult. And without hesitation she said, "Because I am black."

Could it be true that being black was the reason, or one of the reasons? Could be. There is nothing anyone can do about what someone's motives and beliefs are.

However, getting into negotiation with that belief in mind will alter our ability to negotiate or get our point across, because our communication will be overplayed or underplayed in order to account for the belief that we are projecting on the other person.

Becoming aware of this and not doing anything about it allowed Jill to be the creative business woman that she is. The deal closed.

Our neurons are interconnected by trillions of connections called synapses. On average, each connection transmits about one signal per second. Some specialized connections send up to 1,000 signals per second.

Thoughts that are directly triggered by external stimuli such as a feather that brushes your skin, seeing words on a computer screen, or hearing a phone ring, each triggers a series of signals in the brain.

When you read these words, for example, the photons associated with the patterns of the letters hit your retina, and their energy triggers an electrical signal in the light-detecting cells there. That electrical signal propagates like a wave along the long threads called axons that are part of the connections between neurons. When the signal reaches the end of an axon, it causes the release of chemical neurotransmitters into the synapse, a chemical junction between the axon tip and target neurons. A target neuron responds with its own electrical signal, which, in turn, spreads to other neurons. Within a few hundred milliseconds, the signal has spread to billions of neurons in several dozen interconnected areas of your brain, and you have perceived the words. All that, and you probably didn't even break a sweat.

Any thought, any belief that is already stored in our brain, will be recalled and triggered consciously or subconsciously by any piece of information that we are exposed to, and will send us on a journey of remembrance, and not necessarily the pleasant kind, since the brain (the *Identity*) is for the most part trying to protect us. Because the brain is accessing and referencing information that has already been stored, the experience that we have of life is that of repetition; on and on we see the same scenarios, same characters and same emotions, and there is no awareness that there is a reality beyond this one.

From a philosophical point of view, what makes the brain special in comparison to other organs is that it forms the physical structure that generates the mind. Hippocrates said, "Men ought to know that from nothing else but the brain comes joys, delights, laughter, sports, sorrows, grief, despondency, and lamentations."

We believe that we need to make decisions and have all the answers at all times. This is what our need for emotional protection and control demands. We get to protect the other "me" the one we constructed and "represent" us in front of others. That makes sense if we need to physically survive or have to make decisions at work. However, most of us live in such a way that we are not in immediate danger, and we can have the luxury of not making any decisions or have the answer and stay connected with the whole. Not knowing or appearing that we don't know, make us vulnerable.

The challenge is that we try to understand everything through our conscious mind, and within the parameters and demands that the conscious mind has, the demands of the *Identity*, all that we know to be true. We have a mandate or wish to understand and believe that in order for us to really understand anything, we have to have a lifelike intellectual picture of what we are trying to understand. As a consequence, we are walking around with a single picture frame of understanding, trying to fit everything in it. We tear everything so it will fit inside the frame.

We experience sensory overload when we are trying to process consciously all information available as a way to create a safe space for ourselves, and to know where everything is. We try to get as many of those lifelike pictures as we can in order to make sense of our world. We have evolved to process the information that fits in a preconceived reality that is tasking and consuming, that is leaving us no space to Be. **The biggest problem is that we believe that we are in possession of all the facts, therefore all conclusions are believed to be true.**

Left hemisphere tweaks the facts, spins the story and allows us to feel like we're in charge, experiments with split-brain patients reveal.

This is a recount of a walk into the forest and the reaction to a rustling sound.

I hear that rustling in the wind. I jumped, that is, before I was consciously aware that it was the wind that rustled the grass, rather than the rattle. If I had only my conscious processes to depend on, I probably would have jumped less, but been beating on more than one occasion.

Conscious processes are slow, as are conscious decisions. As a person walks, sensory inputs from the visual and auditory systems go to the thalamus, a type of brain relay station. Then the impulses, information, are sent to the processing areas in the cortex, next relayed to the frontal cortex. There they are integrated with other higher mental processes, and perhaps the information makes it into the stream of consciousness, which is when a person becomes consciously aware of the information (there is a snake!) In the case of the rattler, memory then kicks in the information that rattlesnakes are poisonous and what the consequences of a rattlesnakes bite are. I make a decision (I don't want it to bite me), quickly calculate how close I am to the snake, and answer a question: Do I need to change my current direction and speed? Yes, I should move back. A command is set to put the muscles into gear and then they do it.

All this processing takes a long time, up to a second or two. Luckily, all that doesn't have to occur. The brain also takes non-conscious shortcuts through the amygdala, which sits under the thalamus and keeps track of everything. If a pattern associated with danger in the past is recognized by the amygdala, it sends an impulse along a direct connection to the brain stem, which activates the fight -or- flight response and rings the alarm. I automatically jump back before I realize why.

If you were to ask me why I had jumped, I would have replied that I thought I'd seen a snake. The reality, however, is that I jumped way before I was conscious of the snake. My explanation is from post hoc, after the fact information I have in my conscious system.   When I answered that question, I was, in a sense, confabulating, giving a fictitious account of past event, believing it to be true.

I confabulate because our human brains are driven to infer causality. They are driven to make sense out of the scatter facts. The facts that my conscious brain had to work with were that I saw a snake, and I jumped. It did not register that I jumped before I was consciously aware of it.

In truth, when we set out to explain our actions, they are all post hoc, after the fact, explanations using after the fact observation with no access to nonconscious processing. Not only that, our left brain fudges, alters things a bit to fit into a make-sense story. Explanations are all based on what makes it into our consciousness, but actions and the feelings happen before we are consciously aware of them and most of them are the result of nonconscious processes, which will never make it into the explanations. The reality is, listening to people's explanations of their actions is interesting and in the case of politicians entertaining but often a waste of time.

…The right hemisphere, however, does not do this. It is totally veridical only did origin of pi and identifies only the original pictures. The right brain is very literal and doesn't include anything that wasn't there originally. And This is why your three-year old, embarrassingly, will contradict you as you embellish the story. The child's left hemisphere interpreter, which is satisfied with the gist, is not yet fully in gear…

...*Our conscious experiences are assembled on the fly as our brain responds to constantly changing inputs, calculate potential courses of action, and execute responses like a streetwise kid.*

But we don't experience a thousand chattering voices. Consciousness flows easily and naturally from one moment to the next with a single, unified, coherent narrative.

...*Our subjective (Identity) awareness arises out of a dominant left hemisphere's unrelenting quest to explain the bits and pieces that pop into consciousness.*

What does it mean that we built our theories about ourselves after the fact? How much of the time are we confabulating, giving a fictitious account of past events, believing it to be true?

"WHO'S IN CHARGE?" FREE WILL AND THE
SCIENCE OF THE BRAIN
BY MICHAEL S. GAZZANIGA, 2011

SIXTEEN: Consciousness is the Smallest Part of Our Awareness.

...and the child initial universe is entirely centered on his own body and action in an egocentrism as total as it is unconscious (for lack of consciousness of the self). In the course of the first eighteen months, however, there occurs a kind of Copernican revolution, or, more simply, a kind of general decentering process whereby the child eventually comes to regard himself as an object among others in a universe that is made up of permanent objects (that is, structured in a spatio-temporal manner) and in which there is at work a causality that is both localized in space and objectified in things.

THE CONSTRUCTION OF REALITY IN THE
CHILD
BY JEAN PIAGET, 1954

Any thought, any belief that is already stored in our brain, will be recalled and triggered consciously or subconsciously by any piece of information that we are exposed to, and will send us on a journey of remembrance, and not necessarily the pleasant kind, since the brain (the *Identity*) is, for the most part, trying to protect us.

Because the brain is accessing and referencing information that has already been stored, the experience that we have of life is that of repetition; on and on we see the same scenarios, same characters and same emotions, and there is no awareness that there is a reality beyond this one.

We are seeing life, this entire stimulus, and this information as the news headlines, after the fact. The brain process information, we react automatically to the input and then we infer some kind of causality in our actions, or better said, our reactions. It is all after the fact reasoning. We create a whole set of narratives, stories just to fit our actions, in the frame of our beliefs.

When we are pressed to verbalize an answer, we have to frame it within the parameters we are familiar with, and not necessarily within reality.

Alice buys a designer dress for a special event, her best friend's wedding. She arrives to the party feeling beautiful and happy. A lot of old friends are there and they are all happy to see her. They laugh and dance a lot. She is having a great time. Four hours into the party and it has been nonstop fun. Then she stumbles and drops a glass of wine on her beautiful designer dress, staining it.

"This has been the worst day of my life, this ruined the whole party."

The previous four hours are erased and replaced with this statement. This is the memory that will prevail. Maybe she will make up the fact that things are never perfect for her, and because of this she will be looking for bad things to happen in the future even when she is experiencing happiness or success.

All this information is hardwired and stored in our brain, and there is nothing we can do about it unless we discover a way that we can remove the specific brain cells that contain the information and the emotions associated with *our memory* of the facts.

This is all a really complex movie; a virtual world that starts playing without us being aware of it. It feels real and we believe and act as if it is real. No surprise there, why we become reactive and defensive.

How then are we going to be able to experience a different reality other than the one created by our *Identity*, so that we are not reactive and defensive every time those memories are triggered—once the movie is playing loudly and we feel this is the only thing that exists?

Life, as we find it, is too hard for us; it brings us too many pains, disappointments, and impossible tasks. In order to bear it, we cannot dispense with palliative measures. ... There are perhaps three such measures: powerful deflections, which cause us to make light of our misery; substitutive satisfactions, which diminish it; and intoxicating substances, which make us insensitive to it.

CIVILIZATION AND ITS DISCONTENTS
BY SIGMUND FREUD, 1931

Freud is correct if we believe that the brain is "me." With this belief, there is no escape other than to manage our experiences within the confined world of our *Identity*.

A decade or so of neuroscience research has shown without a doubt that the adult brain remains malleable throughout life. The circuits we use most often become stronger and more efficient, areas of the brain they connect become larger, while the ones we don't use shrink and fade away.

As we now know our thoughts, beliefs and emotions are information stored in our brain. This information that we experience as "me" is our *Identity*, the one that negotiates and interprets life for us. We also know that in the isolated world of the *Identity* we experience this to be the universe and the only reality, and there is no other reality. This is it.

Another thing we know is that not every thought the mind produces is based on the reality at hand, and not every thought needs to be attended to.

With these realizations and our continuous awareness of them, the idea of a world outside the *Identity* and its beliefs will start to emerge, creating new neuropaths to store the emerging information, helping us to leave behind the old understanding and beliefs. New neuropaths will be created, eventually developing into a new system where the information is gathered and experienced in the present moment.

This will create a delay that will bring into awareness of a world outside before we take refuge in the universe of the *Identity*, once our old memories are triggered.

This delay is what we are looking for. Now that the system of the *Identity* is not the "go to system," it will start to deteriorate over time. What this means is that the message is still running intact, but the "voice" of its thoughts becomes faint. Also, the delay will allow us to access the other part of our brain, the Being part, or our *essence*, and experience a different reality. Now, the assumed limitations we based our actions on because of the information the *Identity* gathered through the years will not have the same stronghold on our lives that it once had.

The more we bring into awareness the reality outside our *Identity*, the weaker this information will become and the stronger and more complex these new connections will be, especially with the new set of information we receive from the "new system."

Now both systems, the old and the new, will be triggered by the information at hand, and we will be able to make choices moment-to-moment that are more consistent with what we really want.

Do we retreat in fear to the world of the *Identity*, or do we embrace fear as an intrinsic part of being human, remaining present?

SEVENTEEN: Identity

Identity creates a distorted perception of the world and clouds our ability to make distinctions.

The "I" or the *Identity* is a structure and function of the mind. The "I" organizes and interprets external stimulus, assesses and categorizes reality. In its defensive function, it creates the illusion of separateness.

Identity leaves very little space to experience life in real time.

In one of the workshops that I taught at Homeboy Industries, it was very apparent how our *Identity* is the one that represents us, and how difficult it is to give it away.

Stealing from their website www.homeboyindustries.org:

Homeboy Industries provides hope, training, and support to formerly gang-involved and previously incarcerated men and women allowing them to redirect their lives and become contributing members of our community. Each year over

10,000 former gang members from across Los Angeles come through Homeboy Industries' doors in an effort to make a positive change. They are welcomed into a community of mutual kinship, love, and a wide variety of services ranging from tattoo removal to anger management and parenting classes. Full-time employment is offered for more than 200 men and women at a time through an 18-month program that helps them re-identify who they are in the world, and job training is offered so they can move on from Homeboy Industries and become contributing members of the community—knowing they count!

Gina was a hardcore gang member; six-foot-tall in her late thirties, she joined a gang when she was young, so her family and roots were her Barrio (neighborhood).

The challenge that *Thinking in Images* poses is to give up our *Identity*. After the workshop, Gina came to me, and said that she was going to implement what she had learned, but she was not going to remove her barrio tattoo. I was surprised because of her profound understanding of the process and the challenge she was experiencing to give up what she always thought she was. At no point did I give direction on what the people should do or believe. I didn't offer any advice regarding her tattoos, so seeing her becoming so aware was very rewarding.

A month later Gina called me and said, "Alberto I removed my tattoo."

She gave up who she thought she was.

Our challenge is to remove our own tattoos and be aware if we are branding ourselves with new ones.

The "I" or the *Identity*, can be thought of as a variable aspect of the individual constructed as a system of beliefs that organize one's dealings with the internal and external demands of life. It reconciles the biological, instinctual demands and drives, both unifying and destructive in nature, with the socially determined constraints and internalized rules placing limits on the individual's satisfactions and pleasures, and the demands of reality.

The *Identity* is just information that, with time, we identify with and that in adolescence consolidates into "who we are."

The brain can't distinguish between a real threat like someone or something trying to kill us, and an unreal threat like someone who disagrees with our opinion.

The brain sees us as a unit; our thoughts and our physical body are one and the function of the brain is to protect the integrity of both. This is why we are willing to go to war with anyone that attacks our *Identity*, our set of beliefs.

The Art of Swordsmanship.

Toyotomi Hideyoshi was the son of a famous swordsman. His father disowned him thinking that he lacked the qualities of a real swordsman.

Toyotomi sought out the great swordsman Anshin. The latter discouraged him, "You wish to learn swordsmanship from me but you don't have the necessary requirements."

"I'm willing to work hard. How many years do you think it would take for me to become a master?"

"The rest of your life."

"I cannot wait that long. I'm not afraid of hard work. I can put up with anything, only please take me under your tutelage. I'll be your servant and serve you day and night, then how long would it take?"

"...in that case, maybe ten years."

"But soon I'll have to take care of my father, he is getting old. How 'bout if you put me on intensive training, then how long would it take?"

"Thirty years."

"But, you said ten before. I'll do anything to take the shortest time to train. I really mean it."

"Then it will take seventy years. A man in such a hurry as you seldom learns quickly."

Toyotomi had to give up, "Alright, I agree with whatever you say."

From that day on, Toyotomi worked as a servant for Anshin. He cooked his meals. He washed his clothes. He cleaned his house and yard. He cared for his garden. And all the while, Toyotomi was forbidden to speak of fencing or to touch a sword.

Three years passed. Still, Toyotomi did as he was told. But he was sad, thinking that he had no future.

One day, while Toyotomi was working, Anshin sneaked up from behind and struck one terrific blow with his wooden sword. The next day, Anshin did it again. Soon, Anshin's attacks escalated to many times a day, day and night, every day. When his servant was least expecting it, Anshin would attack and give him a taste of his sword!

Toyotomi found himself having to work and at the same time be on guard watching out for his master's unannounced assaults.

"Master, when would I start my swordsmanship training?"

"When you surrender your master."

For a year he tried to avoid his master's attacks, they were painful. He tried to anticipate them, making his life very stressful. He could not anticipate Anshin; he was a Master for a reason. He was miserable and found no purpose whatsoever in his life with Master Anshin. One day after seeing how futile all his efforts were, he decided to surrender to his master's attacks and stopped anticipating him.

When the Master saw this he said, "I see that you surrender to what is. When you anticipate your attacker, you narrow your attention to few possibilities and your life is in danger. When you surrender your mind you become aware of the whole. Now we can start your swordsmanship instruction."

Master gave him a new name, Ansui: Peaceful, calm water. This is how Toyotomi Ansui became the greatest swordsman in the land.

EIGHTEEN: *Identity* vs. Being

I feel the sensation, fight or flight. It's constant. I should just pick one… I Elliot Alderson; I am flight, I am fear, I am anxiety, terror, panic.

ELLIOT ALDERSON, MR. ROBOT
BY SAM ESMAIL

Not knowing or appearing that we don't know make us vulnerable. To avoid appearing weak we constantly make up stuff that resembles reality.

We think in terms of "I" and "mine" we are defined by the boundaries of our bodies and what we own. Our reign extends well beyond the physical realm; we include in it everything we like, everything we believe and the people that make up part of the relationships we create.

We are anthropocentric and this creates an obstacle to understanding things that are not tangible or quantifiable, at least not yet. We like to believe that we are the ones in control, and despite intellectually knowing that this is not true, we constantly try to impose our will on everything we do and all the relationships we are involved in. We are *Being* beings that happen to think, and not thinking beings that happen to be.

We have a great need to place things, to have a reference point, to know where things are in reference to us.

To help you visualize this thing called *Identity*, this thing that we want to break away from, we are going to situate the *Identity* towards the upper part of the back section of our left hemisphere. This is important for the process of altering our perceptions about the mind, the brain and how we can break away from its reality.

This is arbitrary in many ways and at the same time has some validity, since the left side of our brain is the one that is scanning the world at all moments, categorizing things, referencing and alerting us of possible emotional danger by way of fear.

The left hemisphere of the brain functions like a serial processor. Serial processing is processing that occurs sequentially. There is an explicit order in which operations occur, and in general, the results of one action are known before a next action is considered. We string together narratives that have continuity and that support each other to validate our beliefs, our stored information and all the rationalizations we made about them.

The two cerebral cortexes are completely separated from one another. The two hemispheres communicate with one another through the corpus callosum, other than that the two hemispheres are completely separate.

Because they process information differently, each of our hemispheres thinks about different things and they care about different things.

Our left hemisphere thinks linearly and methodically, our left hemisphere is all about the past and is all about the future. Our left hemisphere is designed to take that enormous collage of the present moment and start to pick out details, details and more details about those details, it then categorizes and organizes all the information associates it with everything in the past we ever learned and projects into the future all our possibilities.

The left hemisphere thinks in language, that incessant chatter that connects my internal world to my external world. Is that little voice that says to me; hey, remember to pay your bill. But more important is the voice that says "I am" at that moment I become a separate individual separate from the whole.

MY STROKE OF INSIGHT: A BRAIN SCIENTIST'S
PERSONAL JOURNEY
BY JILL BOLTE TAYLOR, PH. D, 2008

The right hemisphere is all about the here and now. It perceives the whole, and in it, we are connected as one.

When we are "Being" we experience the whole. "Being" does escape the grasp of our intellectual understanding that processes information in a sequential way: cause and effect. This makes our intellect ineffective because it can't grasp a concept that can't be intellectually understood and experienced at the same time.

The intellectual mind tends to process only a few elements at any given time because it has to interpret each one at every step. Being doesn't require an answer.

The right hemisphere, our right brain, functions like a parallel processor. In computers, parallel processing is the processing of programming instructions that divide them among multiple processors with the objective of running a program in less time.

In the brain, parallel processing is the ability of the brain to simultaneously process incoming stimuli of differing quality. What this means is that the right hemisphere processes different information at the same time without following a storyline.

As Dr. Jill Bolte Taylor puts it: "Our right hemisphere is all about this present moment, all about the here right now. Our right hemisphere thinks in pictures and learns kinesthetically through the movement of our body. We experience connection with the whole, we are connected with one another and we experience being one human family when experiencing life from the right hemisphere".

This *Identity*, this system of neurons at the top of the left side of our brain (this is an arbitrary place to help you relate with it), is a depository of information about people, events, what we made up about the events, what we made up about what we made up, a collection of learned emotions, decisions, about others, about ourselves, about life. Everything that we came to believe and is real to us.

The system of the *Identity* is made out of brain cells that are interconnected to transport and store information. When we are young, the system is not as complex. As we get older, we start either bringing more of the same information that strengthens old connections or we make up new stuff about the old stuff that creates more connections.

When the brain is scanning, it will scan for familiar information and it will zero in to validate the information we already have and confirm our suspicions. This is why events and experiences get repeated in our lives. It is difficult to attend to anything else when we are focused on looking for what is familiar.

For the person who is jealous, any sudden move of her partner will be interpreted as inappropriate and will justify her actions by validating her belief that she will be cheated on.

Within the system of the *Identity*, there is always need to be certain, reality will be broken in pieces to accommodate information in such a way that it makes sense to the *Identity*.

Thinking in Images is about acknowledging the *Identity* for what it is; a system of information that has the job of protecting me from emotional pain, and allow myself to experience life without the need of an answer, of referencing or predicting the future. The *Identity* is all about the past and the future.

People with the means to otherwise travel, don't move to a different town or city, or get into a different relationship remaining in the same conditions because there is no awareness of another world other than the one presented by their *Identity*. In this world, there is no awareness that they are not confined by their parent's orders or limited by the boundaries of their room, that they actually have bank accounts or have cars to take a drive. The power of what we believe to be true is stronger than reality.

Remember Peter B., the scientist whose parents showed him little attention after his young sister's death, making him question if he, in fact, had anything of value to offer to anyone?

At work he procrastinated until either someone demanded for the job to be done or pushed him into leadership position. Although all the evidence showed that everyone looked up to him, even senior employees, he did just enough and sometimes even less, believing that there was no point to anything because there is no way to know things would work. He was not aware of the qualities he had developed and that his decisions were based on a worldview of the powerless 5, 6, 7... years old boy he was.

His personal relationships were the same, although he had a woman clearly interested in him. He asked her if she wanted to go out with him, she said yes and then he never calls her. The expectation was for her to tell him to move forward, again living his life with no power of decision. Although he owns a car and a motorcycle he spent his days in his apartment turning down invitations from friends.

We all at some point live our lives as if we are powerless kids with no options. This doesn't mean we are immature, it means that the only information we are accessing is what is provided by our minds, and at that moment we believe it to be the universe to us. What makes it more problematic is that afterwards, we rationalize our actions, "making sense" of what we did or said.

A client who happens to be a scientist and is very willing to do the work, when she was pressed with elementary logic to illustrate her thought process, claimed ignorance and no amount of simple examples sufficed to help her see the cause and effect of her actions.

She claimed ignorance before challenging and experiencing separation from her *Identity*.

We experience separation from the *Identity* as immense fear, as if we are going to physically die.

NINETEEN: Avoiding Pain and Fear: How the Identity Consolidates Its Role

My soul is like a hidden orchestra; I do not know which instruments grind and play away inside of me, strings and harps, timbales and drums. I can only recognize myself as a symphony.

THE BOOK OF DISQUIET
BY FERNANDO PESSOA, 1984

We have a mandate or wish to understand and believe that in order for us to really understand anything, we have to have a lifelike intellectual picture of what we are trying to understand. As a consequence, we are walking around with a single picture frame of understanding, trying to fit everything in it. We tear everything so it will fit inside the frame.

The nature of the *Identity* and the relationship that we have created with it makes it very difficult for us to depart from it. The relationship has been so close that to think of a life without it is inconceivable, or so we think. Even when the concept of the *Identity* function is accepted, the immediate reaction is, "How am I going to know what to do?"

What we have not realized is that the statement, "How am I going to know what to do?" is not about how to do things. We know what to do automatically when the situation arises, all the practical knowledge that we have accumulated doesn't go anywhere. It is information that we have stored and is available at all times.

What we would be missing is the need to reference our emotions and the subsequent need of protection. Without this interference, we are able to experience the world as something to be discovered every moment, instead of expecting what has been familiar and predicting events before they happen, and therefore having our attention focused on our expectations, missing out on everything else. This way we will experience others without the emotional history that we and the *Identity* have stored.

The chatter of the mind is incessant, and we learn to believe that the voice is our own "voice" and that we are producing it. Anyone that thinks that this is not so will be considered some kind of insane.

As a consequence of this belief, we resolve the conflict of inconsistency with general statements that consolidate the information that the beliefs the *Identity* have stored, therefore: *men/women are not to be trusted, bad things always happen to me, people are jealous of me, etc.*

Alberto: when you say the critic came out and blew up everything, what do you mean by that?

Peter B: What do I mean by that? It just is like the benefits that I am doing for myself getting sleep or whatever are too little too late. Is eight hours of sleep really going to make up for the last twenty years of me spinning around and not doing my best, and sort of falling behind, not getting the Ph.D. and everything else in my life? Is eight hours of sleep, going to give me a girlfriend? After eight hours of sleep I'm still three hundred pounds.

A: The problem that you have is not that you weigh three hundred pounds, it is not that you can't sleep away all these things that you mention that you have not been able to fulfill. The problem that you have is that voice you were just talking about. The voice that is complaining and bringing all your history into right here and right now. Therefore somehow you think that the voice cannot be silenced, you trust that voice to describe reality for you. The only way to silence it is for you to drop to two hundred pounds and to have your ideal results right here, right now.

The reality is that the voice tells you, "You don't matter enough to have what you want when you want it." There is nothing you can do about that voice other than acknowledge it as the voice of the *Identity*, something that you are not.

If you don't do anything to your diet and go to the gym just once, you will lose a few grams of weight. It may not be that great compared to all the weight you want to lose. However, if you combine that with a little change in your diet and do this consistently, you will start to experience the changes in your body that you were looking for, even if in between you fail to follow your own directions.

But we all know that consistency will get you there. However, wherever you want to go, you can't do it instantly. You start walking and keep walking one step at a time, and you get there when you get there. In between steps, it is up to us to decide whether to listen to the voice and take a detour, hiding out in the predictable world of the *Identity*, or acknowledge the voice and the emotions that come with it, and do nothing about them. A few things may happen; you may slow down, you may stop completely or you may fail. Either way, you are participating in your life.

The thing that doesn't allow you to look at that logic is the voice that is telling you, "Hey, nothing that you do matters." And when you experience that voice from within the *Identity*, all the evidence that has been gathered throughout your life will support that belief, and you will feel drained, sleepy, have no energy and you will give up, no other reality will be experienced.

The reality is that the *Identity* keeps these records ready and available to be referenced when we fail, like a box of papers that we carry under our arm as evidence of our failing and we don't put this box down. The evidence is there, being broadcast loudly. The imagery is rich, and yet it is not the only reality. The only thing you need to do is question it. Questioning will stop the process. It will interrupt the flow of information and it will take you out of that universe. You already know where you want to be and how to get there. This thing in between is the one that is in the way, the chaos that is experienced when the world is a menacing thing and we run for cover trying to avoid fear and pain. Not much that is new can be learned when we are in survival mode.

Now the voice that is telling you all that stuff will keep telling you that it is never going to go away. But if you question it, "Hold on a second, did I fail? Yes. Do I feel fear or pain? Yes. Could I feel these emotions and do nothing about them, and nothing would happen to me? Yes. Does this mean that this moment is permanent? No. Is this the only reality I live in? No. So in the next moment, I could do what I want to and it would be ok? Yes.

That is enough information to start building a new system that will compete with the one in place, and you will be doing the things that you want more often than not. The voice with time will be less loud at some point, it will be become a distant whisper.

You make your life moment to moment; this moment doesn't have any memory of the previous one only the *Identity* and you do.

If something is thrown unexpectedly in our direction, the response would be automatic. Let's say a ball is thrown towards you, the reaction would be to interfere with the trajectory or catch it.

What happens is the brain picks up information through our senses (sight, hearing, taste, smell, touch) and then makes a decision based on that information, sending commands to other parts of your body that eventually has the muscles of your arm contract and extend to catch that ball before it hits you. The brain is doing all this before you are consciously aware of it. The brain is not thinking, "Who threw that ball and what color is it?" The brain senses danger in the approaching object and sprints into action. We consolidate the story of the event by rationalizing, "I saw a ball coming in my direction and I decided to catch it before it hits me." However, that is an afterthought designed to make sense of our actions, and to bring balance to our life in which we are in control of our actions and thoughts and we are at the center of things.

Our need to be at the center of our world, unifying reality with our *Identity*, creates conflict and clashes with everything that is already there.

Josh is a busy professional, and recently his father passed away. He now has to take care of some family affairs for his now widowed mother with whom he has a contemptuous relationship. In addition to this, his daughter is now living with him and she has been diagnosed with ADD, depression and anxiety.

This is in his words what happened:

Josh: I was totally high jacked this morning and didn't even realize it. And it is weird because I can look back on it and kind of justify it, or try to say, "Well it needed to happen and in the end it kind of resolved itself," or, "It came to a resolution that I think is good, but it didn't need to happen the way it happened." And it was totally me being in reaction mode and angry and, and I, just... anger rearing its ugly head again.

A: And when you say it rears its ugly head again, what do you mean by that?

J: Well, you know the anger, and the reaction, and the lack of control and then the I need to be right, and justifying and excusing and all the stuff that I do to stay safe in my, you know, in my *Identity* of, "Don't you know I will not be tested or argued, I am right."

A: Ok, could you tell me a little bit about the incident?

J: Well, Lisa, my daughter, she has not been feeling really well. She's had a little bit of a sore throat, that's what she told me. When I got her up to go to school this morning I couldn't tell, are you sick or are you just trying to get out of going to school. I couldn't control my emotions about it. I got angry and I got bitter.

A: Ok, we are not going to look at the events as you describe or analyze them since this is the result and not the source of something. We are not reliable witnesses, sometimes we exonerate ourselves and sometimes we condemn ourselves, and most times the words we use are related with the emotional value we placed on our experiences. Besides, there is no need for you to be sentenced, it doesn't contribute one bit to our ultimate goal.

She is doing something, and you feel angry and feel bitter. Those were the words that you used. Your description of what is real to you.

J: Right.

A: It's not about correcting or rephrasing what you said or anything like that. That's what it was, that is what you said and for you that is what is real. Whether your description is true or not doesn't matter.

Let's see what happened, what got you to become angry. In your mind, she is trying to get away with something.

J: Yes! Oh yes, and that is exactly where I went.

A: That may be true, let's say it is 100% true that she is trying to get away with something.

So she is trying to get away with something and you at that moment don't feel in control. You feel out of control and the way you react is panicking. When you panic, you get angry as most of us do. We get scared and we don't want to be scared, so instead we become angry. Anger is what we use to save ourselves from experiencing the fear and the pain and/or the possibility of pain we experience when there is a situation we don't have control over.

If we were ok feeling scared or in pain, then there would be no need for anger.

Does it make sense so far?

J: Yes, yes.

A: That's what it was and that is all it was. You felt scared and didn't like the experience of that feeling, instead, you became angry.

Fear is physical and mental sensations that alert us of imminent danger. Is telling us that something that happened before may happen again, so you better be watchful. Fear forecasts the possibility or certainty of pain.

Also being afraid is something that has been equated with weakness, and we don't want to appear weak, absolutely not!

The practice at that moment is for you to acknowledge that you are either scared or in pain; you could be both, most probably you are both, and do nothing about it. What this means is that you always can go back to the situation and talk it over. It is important to realize that it could be resolved at a later time.

The thing is that you are not hurt or scared by the situation that is happening right now. What is happening is that the way you see the situation right now is beyond your perceived capability for control, so you react with fear and panic as if you don't have the tools to deal with the present events in a different way.

J: Ok...

A: Let's look back on the life of Joe, we don't even need to go to the places where events that were impactful took place. You will do that in another session if necessary. You don't need to go the exact places and moments, for now.

You are going to go there anyway on your own as you arrive to some realizations.

So what happened was this: at some point in your life in the period you were forming and creating your reality as it was, including memories, events, what you came to believe is true to you, there were recurrent situations in which you experienced your world being out of your control.

The way you have this information stored in your brain is in the context and with the content that was present at that time, when you were 2, 3, 4, 5-year-old boy that you once were. So when these emotions are triggered the brain references those memories with the information it has stored, and here you are high jacked by your brain and you are responding as a 2, 3, 4, or 5-year-old with his limited abilities trying to resolve a situation that to the eyes of the little kid is out of control and the kid doesn't have any power over what is happening. It is pretty scary and pretty hurtful.

Of course, it is pretty scary reliving those moments that also trigger pain.

Because these memories are triggers, we relive our memories and the pain is also relieved.

The pain and fear are experienced physically, the pressure on your chest and/or the feeling in the pit of your stomach is real, and your mind is telling you, "Hey, right now the possibility of something that hurt you in the past happening again is pretty high, so you better be watchful."

Again, we set ourselves up to find evidence for the pain and the evidence for the fear right here, right now with the eyes of a 5-year-old kid.

Now with that pain and fear being experienced, we assume it is caused by what is happening in the present moment.

We can make people pay dearly for causing us pain.

This is why you reacted to your daughter the way you did. Not because you are a bad father, not because you are just an angry S.O.B., not because you are a selfish S.O.B., none of that. That is an intellectualization we human beings have created, a long history of rationalizing our emotions so we have some kind of intellectual understanding of our behavior. We can't compartmentalize our emotions. We are either retreating to our *Identity*, our thoughts and beliefs, or we are "Being" in that moment. Categories are given "after the fact."

We created all these categories, these shades that we use to describe our emotions to give us some sense of understanding and control.

This is neither right nor wrong, it is what it is.

Now the thing that hooks you and creates an insane loop is that you are a good man, and you come to realize that you shouldn't have behaved as you did, and so you beat the heck out of yourself. You punished yourself for the acts you committed.

Now you are in real trouble because now you have come to some realization that you caused pain and fear in someone you love. Now you are in more pain, for having inflicted pain, and you also don't want to experience this pain either so you become angrier at yourself and at your daughter for "making" you do what you did.

This is why your progress has been so slow to overcome these emotions and alter your behavior.

There is nothing to do about what you did as unfortunate as it was. However, if you come to realize that you panicked, that you felt betrayed, and that your daughter happened to be there and that interaction was quickly referenced to events in your past, experiencing them subconsciously, and the only possible way for you to feel and cope with the present situation was with information your *Identity* was providing, you may be able to experience a different new information that will help you to be and relate differently in similar situation.

As you experience life in such limited space, you have very limited tools to deal with life. You probably have a single tool and it is a hammer. If you acknowledge that you are scared and you are willing to be comfortable being uncomfortable, then you don't need to reach for the hammer. Let yourself be scared, there will be another moment after this. You won't die, do nothing about it. Let her "get away with it," let yourself be scared, and let yourself be hurt.

Now you will start to have an awareness of the other parts of you that were out of sight because all your efforts and resources were devoted to protect you from pain and fear. Letting pain and fear be your "guests" allows you become available to your resources and your resources to be available to you. Now that you have become functional, it is not going to be perfect because you have not practiced enough to be familiar with all your resources, and fear is very scary. But now that you can generate life rather than react to life, you will have a say in your life.

This is way better than using the hammer. Your daughter now can start to emerge as who she is, not the reflection of your inadequacies, and you can relate with her as her father and she as the unique lady that she is. You both will get to discover each other in this lifetime process.

As you do this time and then again, you become more resourceful, therefore more peaceful. At some point, the two of you are going to create a different kind of relationship.

The changes will become permanent as the new information is creating new neuropaths to compete with the old ones.

She is going to have a space to breathe. She is scared and she has picked up a lot of things, including behaviors from you with no content.

Here is your kid that grows up around a father who is depressed and angry. The kid has no idea what is going on with you, she just knows your behavior and demeanor. What she will learn is to mimic in some way these behaviors and figure out how to mesh them with the ones that she has developed. She will learn to look the part; the only thing missing is content for that depression. The mind needs to make sense of everything we do, so she will make up some thoughts around these learned behaviors that will justify them. A kid can make up the fact that nobody likes them, or misbehave to accomplish the same result. This is now incorporated in her *Identity* and becomes the real world to her. From this point on it is all about how to prove this to be true. She will learn to cope with reality defensively, and she will feel she doesn't have any control, and will react with panic to any challenge she encounters. It will make life difficult to deal with since she will have only a hammer as her parents did to resolve conflict.

J: What can I do to change it?

A: We always jump and try to find the solution to our suffering. We don't want to suffer, that is probably our biggest obstacle, and in trying to keep us safe from suffering we lock everything out; we lock out life itself. We must realize that we can't do anything about what already happened except understand it for what it was.

You will come up with resolutions that will surprise you. That is a process that will consolidate with time, you will act from wisdom, rather than from knowing.

We normally try to cope with these kinds of situations by feeling resentment or anger again. Resentment is, "I shouldn't have done that." It will keep you with your face against the wall that is keeping pain and fear out. What you get to do is experience hurt, and the pain of causing pain and that is all. Feel sad if you do, but there is no need to attach any other meaning to it.

There is no judgment involved, judgment is you looking back, unwilling to be with the pain you caused. There will be another moment to do something, to be different.

You could realize now that if you could have been then the man you are discovering now, things would have been different. And that would be a great distinction. Now you can act differently. The man that you are now can be manifest in your actions. Do not make up for what you did, BE who you have become. Don't bring people back to who you were there to satisfy your own needs, making them responsible for your pain. People want the real you now, that is why they choose you to begin with.

We have lived believing that we are our brains, that the *Identity* I helped co-created is who I am, therefore the only reality I experience is the one my brain provides. The reality is that the brain is computing information on its own and we tag along after the fact.

The way we relate to the information the brain is providing will change, realizing that it is not the only reality available, and as a consequence, we will have options available that will support what we really want in life. It will help you to give way to the qualities you know you possess, but have not been able to exercise, at least as often as you would like.

The practice is to realize that at any moment that you choose anger is a way to cope with chaos because you feel out of control, and you feel that you are not empowered to deal with the situation at hand. That someone may or will take advantage of you.

Again, you don't need to think about that in those terms, be ok being in pain and being scared and not knowing why. It is ok not to resolve the problem immediately. Whatever your daughter is doing, she is not doing it to you; she is just doing what she is doing.

Now if you find yourself all the way in it reacting, angry, and you realize it, just stop and say to yourself, "Something may be hurting or scaring me and it is ok for me to experience pain and fear. Let me feel this and let me not reach for the hammer. Let's see what comes into my awareness." Let the pain and fear be guests, let them come in. You probably will have an eye on them, but your world won't disappear by trying to hold them out.

This is not a miracle cure, although the cure could be miraculous if you practice constantly and consistently.

This is fundamental in the process to alter our relationship with our brain.

At the moment we are just identifying things. *Thinking in Images* for the most part doesn't connect things for you, that will make them intellectually understood. We don't want that. Instead, you will make the connections at a more profound level as you detach from the *Identity*, in a more impactful way than either of us could do intellectually.

TWENTY: Bringing to the Foreground What was Indistinguishable in the Background.

Self-actualizing persons' contact with reality is simply more direct. And along with this unfiltered, unmediated directness of their contact with reality comes also a vastly heightened ability to appreciate again and again, freshly and naively, the basic goods of life, with awe, pleasure, wonder, and even ecstasy, however stale those experiences may have become for others.

TOWARD A PSYCHOLOGY OF BEING BY
ABRAHAM MASLOW 1968

When the stored memories and experiences are triggered, most of the time we are not conscious of it. We experience the world to be only the emotions and thoughts that have been triggered. In some cases, people say, "I was blinded by anger," which holds a lot of truth. When we are experiencing only our thoughts, life becomes menacing because there is no other reality available and there is no way out. We get just bits and parts of information and we just look for evidence, the reason for our emotions in the present moment to complete the picture.

Imagine that your mind, the *Identity*, the part in charge of stringing together your beliefs, the one that gives you the sense of *Identity* is a tent or crystal vase. This is your hard drive, a sophisticated hard drive. The inside of this tent, this crystal vase is the only reality you are able to experience, you have no awareness that other world exists. Since this *Identity* is constantly scanning the world for what is familiar, it usually finds it and consequently triggers the memories that have the elements that the *Identity* can reference, that are found to be similar to the reality at hand. Once it finds it, this becomes the reality we experience and it is like the tent, the crystal vase, the *Identity* descends over ourselves and the only thing that we experience as real are images, thoughts, projected on its walls. Pretty overwhelming feeling.

For many years, day after day I got up in the morning with a gripping feeling in the pit of my stomach, a feeling of dread. A little while after starting the day depression settled in and permeated every aspect of my life.

When I was a kid, it was very difficult to focus or stay still for periods of time when I was surrounded by people. I was able to stay still for hours staring at the sky when I was alone but not at school. Also I had great difficulty with classes that included concepts I could not visualize, and had a great feeling of uneasiness seeing the other kids understanding it while I did not. Proximity made me jumpy and uncomfortable, well more than uncomfortable—I felt invaded and attacked. This made me prone to fights. Because of all this, I was called to be disciplined constantly in the classroom for being disruptive, outside the classroom for fighting, and at home for having bad grades and everything I did inside and outside the classroom. During my time in Colombia there was no timeout, it was belt time.

So you can imagine that starting the day wasn't that exciting for me. Well, I didn't know until much later what the nature of those emotions was.

The mornings from Monday through Thursday and Sunday nights were always accompanied with a feeling of sadness in the pit of my stomach.

I didn't know what was happening back then, I placed those emotions with my other inadequacies without questioning it and did what everyone does to bring some sense of unity: get angry, short tempered, get hurt very easily, blame others, be smarter and more opinionated than others, control conversations to appease myself, telling myself that I was not good, believing that others were not good, pushing relationships away, drinking, etc. I saw the world, or what I thought the world was, as a scary place. So I disengaged, I was depressed. I could not sort out all the information, I had anxiety and panic attacks and felt isolated in my own mind. I experienced life within the confines of the tent of the *Identity*, trapped with the movies of the many memories projected on its walls and the incessant chatter that muffled any other sound.

Because of the difficulty, I have in understanding certain subjects as they are taught in school these emotions intensified in College and University (this is one of the reasons I decided to teach myself rather than going back to formal schooling).

Through a lot of work, some things started to fall in the appropriate places one step at a time, to the point where the feeling in the pit of my stomach of sadness stood alone without much interpretation. Only the feeling remained, contributing to my depression. At this point, I still looked for evidence that validated those emotions in the present moment. It took some time to start to realize that the emotion was bound with those early years.

It was scary to go to school and the grey skies and the early hours were associated with so many unpleasant situations and difficulties. Fear was a regular part of life. Sundays were dreadful; I hated going back to school.

As I grew older, the emotions were triggered by early hours and gray skies, and Sunday nights were the anticipation of that cycle again. At age forty, I used to have a Sunday feeling as if I had not done homework, 30 years after finishing elementary school.

However, before I got to see this for what it was, I felt scared and sad and then I looked for evidence why I felt this way, sometimes blaming others around me.

When I felt this way my only reality was one of my thoughts and emotions, and I looked for evidence from within the context of the information I had at the moment. Here I had no awareness of life outside my thoughts. Only after I acknowledged the nature of the emotions and embraced them did a reality outside my *Identity* become available, I realized and I was functional and available and I started to see the world as less threatening than before.

Embracing the fear and pain triggered by those memories was a slow process. Many times when I was deep into reacting, and looking for the source of my fears and pain in the present moment created a lot of stress and anxiety. A lot of decisions were made that cost me pain and caused pain to others either by my actions or lack thereof.

There was nothing I could do about the emotions. Acknowledging them for what they were helped release my grasp on that reality and I saw them for what they truly are: automatic responses to a memory. No different than when you see a sad movie.

Not reacting will give us a new relationship with events in our life and in time we will gather enough evidence and new information that we will address events differently than we did before. This is a direct result of making the distinction from what is in your head and what is outside; the result will be experiencing life in the present.

Engaging doesn't mean not being afraid, it means being present, staying engaged. What this will do with time is allow you to see things for what they are and create a different relationship with fear and pain. This way you will become more comfortable staying present without the need to escape reality for the familiar world of the *Identity*, trading possibilities for certainty.

In the mid-'90s, the CDC and Kaiser Permanente discovered an exposure that dramatically increased the risk for seven out of 10 of the leading causes of death in the United States. In high doses, it affects brain development, the immune system, hormonal systems, and even the way our DNA is read and transcribed. Folks who are exposed to very high doses have triple the lifetime risk of heart disease and lung cancer and a 20-year difference in life expectancy. Now, the exposure I'm talking about is not a pesticide or a packaging chemical. It's childhood trauma...

I am talking about threats that are so severe or pervasive that they literally get under our skin and change our physiology: things like abuse or neglect, or growing up with a parent who struggles with mental illness or substance dependence.

Now, for a long time, I viewed these things in the way I was trained to view them, either as a social problem -- refer to social services -- or as a mental health problem -- refer to mental health services. And then something happened to make me rethink my entire approach. When I finished my residency, ... I came to work for California Pacific Medical Center, one of the best private hospitals in Northern California, and together, we opened a clinic in Bayview-Hunters Point, one of the poorest, most underserved neighborhoods in San Francisco... We targeted the typical health disparities: access to care, immunization rates, asthma hospitalization rates, and we hit all of our numbers. We felt very proud of ourselves.

But then I started noticing a disturbing trend. A lot of kids were being referred to me for ADHD, or Attention Deficit Hyperactivity Disorder, but when I actually did a thorough history and physical, what I found was that for most of my patients, I couldn't make a diagnosis of ADHD. Most of the kids I was seeing had experienced such severe trauma that it felt like something else was going on. Somehow I was missing something important.

Now, before I did my residency, I did a master's degree in public health, and one of the things that they teach you in public health school is that if you're a doctor and you see 100 kids that all drink from the same well, and 98 of them develop diarrhea, you can go ahead and write that prescription for dose after dose after dose of antibiotics, or you can walk over and say, "What the hell is in this well?" So I began reading everything that I could get my hands on about how exposure to adversity affects the developing brains and bodies of children.

And then one day, my colleague walked into my office, and he said, "Dr. Burke, have you seen this?" In his hand was a copy of a research study called the Adverse Childhood Experiences Study. That day changed my clinical practice and ultimately my career.

The Adverse Childhood Experiences Study is something that everybody needs to know about. It was done by Dr. Vince Felitti at Kaiser and Dr. Bob Anda at the CDC, and together, they asked 17,500 adults about their history of exposure to what they called "adverse childhood experiences," or ACEs. These include physical, emotional, or sexual abuse; physical or emotional neglect; parental mental illness, substance dependence, incarceration; parental separation or divorce; or domestic violence. For every yes, you would get a point on your ACE score. And then what they did was they correlated these ACE scores against health outcomes. What they found was striking. Two things: Number one, ACEs are incredibly common. Sixty-seven percent of the population had at least one ACE, and 12.6 percent, one in eight, had four or more ACEs. The second thing that they found was that there was a dose-response relationship between ACEs and health outcomes: the higher your ACE score, the worse your health outcomes. For a person with an

ACE score of four or more, their relative risk of chronic obstructive pulmonary disease was two and a half times that of someone with an ACE score of zero. For hepatitis, it was also two and a half times. For depression, it was four and a half times. For suicidality, it was 12 times. A person with an ACE score of seven or more had triple the lifetime risk of lung cancer and three and a half times the risk of ischemic heart disease, the number one killer in the United States of America.

Well, of course, this makes sense. Some people looked at this data and they said, "Come on. You have a rough childhood, you're more likely to drink and smoke and do all these things that are going to ruin your health. This isn't science. This is just bad behavior."

It turns out this is exactly where the science comes in. We now understand better than we ever have before how exposure to early adversity affects the developing brains and bodies of children. It affects areas like the nucleus accumbens, the pleasure and reward center of the brain that is implicated in substance dependence. It inhibits the prefrontal cortex, which is necessary for impulse control and executive function, a critical area for learning. And on MRI scans, we see measurable differences in the amygdala, the brain's fear response center. So there are real neurologic reasons why folks exposed to high doses of adversity are more likely to engage in high-risk behavior, and that's important to know.

But it turns out that even if you don't engage in any high-risk behavior, you're still more likely to develop heart disease or cancer. The reason for this has to do with the hypothalamic–pituitary– adrenal axis, the brain's and body's stress response system that governs our fight-or-flight response. How does it work? **Well, imagine you're walking in the forest and you see a bear. Immediately, your hypothalamus sends a signal to your pituitary, which sends a signal to your adrenal gland that says, "Release stress hormones! Adrenaline! Cortisol!" And so your heart starts to pound, Your pupils dilate, your airways open up, and you are ready to either fight that bear or run from the bear. And that is wonderful if you're in a forest and there's a bear.**

But the problem is what happens when the bear comes home every night, and this system is activated over and over and over again, *and it goes from being adaptive, or life-saving, to maladaptive, or health-damaging. Children are especially sensitive to this repeated stress activation, because their brains and bodies are just developing. High doses of adversity not only affect brain structure and function, they affect the developing immune system, developing hormonal systems, and even the way our DNA is read and transcribed.*

So for me, this information threw my old training out the window, because when we understand the mechanism of a disease, when we know not only which pathways are disrupted, but how, then as doctors, it is our job to use this science for prevention and treatment. That's what we do.

HOW CHILDHOOD TRAUMA AFFECTS HEALTH
ACROSS A LIFETIME
BY DR NADINE BURKE HARRIS

TWENTY-ONE: What is Real (?)

....in the absence of a center or origin, everything became discourse...

STRUCTURE, SIGN, AND PLAY IN THE
DISCOURSE OF HUMAN SCIENCES
BY JACQUES DERRIDA, 1970

The menu is not the meal.

ALAN W. WATTS

To write about Antonin Artaud, the work (of) Antonin Artaud, the madness of Antonin Artaud, is not to talk of Antonin Artaud. "when I say Zen, is not Zen what I am talking about". And is not those words found in his writings expressed by a certain Antonin Artaud the ones that give us the Being-Antonin Artaud.

MADNESS AND TRUTH: MAP OF (AN)
ANTONIN ARTAUD
BY RENÉ SUÁREZ, 2004

By breaking the possibility of a narrative, the individual thinks in images, creating a definite distinction between memories and reality as it is happening now, in the present moment.

We don't need to add up to the movie the *Identity* projects, by letting it play we will experience the moment in real time.

Language help us among other things to string a narrative that takes into an account the past and future, the narratives build on their selves creating a story and eliciting subdivisions of emotions that appeal to the intellect of the narrator and with the right audience, to the listener to create a shared reality and a set of invented emotions.

When incoming stimulation is perceived as familiar, the amygdala is calm and the adjacently position hippocampus is capable of learning and memorizing new information. However, as soon as the amygdala is triggered by unfamiliar or perhaps threatening stimulation it raises the brains level of anxiety and focuses the mind attention on the immediate situation. Under the circumstances, our attention is shifted away from the hippocampus and focus toward self-preserving behavior about the present moment. Sensory information streams in through our sensory systems and is immediately processed through our limbic system by the time the message reaches our cerebral cortex for higher thinking we have already placed a feeling upon how we view that stimulation: is this pain or is this pleasure.

"MY STROKE OF INSIGHT" A BRAIN SCIENTIST'S PERSONAL JOURNEY BY JILL BOLTE TAYLOR, PH. D, 2008

How these basic emotions play out in our lives and how our relationship with them affects us depends on our ability to identify them for what they are and not to act on them. The brain takes in the information through our senses and it warns us that events will repeat. The basic emotions are fear, pain or fear of pain.

The first realization we have about those basic emotions takes place in our early years, and because these emotions are so impactful they are stored with all the elements present in the context of the events at the time they were taking place. Because of this, when the brain picks up information it immediately references it against these early memories, triggering them. Then we subconsciously relive them. The subconscious experience is feeling as if they are happening again. There is no distinction between the memory and the present moment. As we experience them and live them again, we experience them in the original context with original content in the original time. In it we are 1, 2, 3, 4, 5, or 6 years old with a limited ability to deal with conflict or chaos.

Normally kids panic, cry, throw a tantrum, act up, or become aggressive, all with the same purpose of resolving the cause of anxiety.

Now, since reality for us at that moment is the memory we are reliving as a child, this is how we deal with the problem at hand in the present moment, with the abilities and common sense of that kid. The only difference is that we have bigger "guns;" all of what we have learned over the years, how to argue and fight, all that we learned about other's weaknesses are used by the "child" so they can get what they want—to alleviate the cause of anxiety and the uneasy feeling of not being in control.

Throughout our evolution, societies as they became wealthier and more evolved placed a great emotional value to other things other than physical survival, such as saving face. This information becomes hard wired in our brains by the support of everyone around us that share the same reality, and we quickly become reactive to anybody challenging these beliefs. We now experience these beliefs as if they are as solid and real as our body or limbs are.

Our brain is wired to react when our emotional buttons are pushed (when we are threatened). We retain the ability to react to incoming stimulation in the original context in which it was recorded. This is why we often react towards our siblings or parents as if we were young kids with disregard or knowledge that we have the ability or the means to act and react differently.

These are Peter B, and Francis from previous Chapters:

Peter B, grew up unable to make decisions on his own, and have difficulty connecting emotionally with his parents; played video games for hours alone in his room to avoid the chaos in his life. Now a professional living alone, copes with life by watching movies for hours.

As a kid he was confined to his room, he had no power of decision. He couldn't say, "I am going out and I'll go wherever pleases me." Now with grown up toys, car, a motorcycle and money, he watches Netflix for hours, and in his mind he has no choice. As he has expressed constantly, he thinks his life sucks.

Francis had an abusive father. Her life was extremely stressful. At one point when she was a young teenager her father was being abusive with her mom and she pulled a knife on her father. The chaotic life raised her level of anxiety and put her in a permanent state of alertness. Anything could trigger these memories and emotions. One of the ways she used to handle the anxiety of the uncertainty was to clean for hours until her fingers were bleeding. This helped her to focus on something and have everything away somehow mitigating the chaos of her thoughts. As a grownup she shielded herself from relationships, demanding the closeness that she herself was not able or willing to grant, and she equated relationships with chaos and emotional pain.

Embracing Fear and Pain

Fear and pain are the basic emotions that we experience most frequently. We experience them often and most of the time we are not aware that we are actually experiencing them or we are unwilling to acknowledge that we are experiencing them.

At the moment of these events, at an early age, the experience is terrifying since it gives us a view of a world that is chaotic, a world in which we are powerless. Our reluctance to experiencing pain has to do with the fact that pain is associated with past events that at the moment were very painful emotionally and sometimes physically.

From the child's perspective the world as she knows it, what was familiar, has disappeared or transformed into something unrecognizable. It created a chaotic sense of the world where we experience ourselves not having control or a way out. And we don't have a way out, a child can't take her car and drive away; we have no options.

We don't rationalize our parents' actions as they are being abusive and say, "Dad is a really unreasonable person, there's no way to have him understand that I have more important things to do. I better go and rest." We instead internalized our parents' actions and in many cases, we *become* the cause of it. "What is wrong with me that my mom and dad treat me this way? I do deserve this treatment."

Often these events repeat over and over again because the source of this chaotic and unpredictable world are the people that are closest to us—our parents, sibling, relatives or neighbors, and these people are battling their own conflicts, they are coping with their own deficiencies with consistent patterns.

Each of us has their own example of what has been consistent in their life. Some others had events of physical or sexual abuse that also brought the sense of chaos in their lives, and although they may not have been repeated, because of the intrusive nature of these events, they created a deep impression that put the child in a permanent state of alert, so that the child doesn't experience the world as a safe place anymore.

I am not my Brain

We all probably have all had an interaction with someone in our lives that is so disjointed that it seemed to be like both are talking two different languages. This has to do more with the "movie" or the "holodeck" projection than with you at that moment. Your friend is probably reacting to you as you are the character or characters in his movie. You are superimposed on the movie he is experiencing or reliving in that moment, and he is superimposed on yours.

Now, what about the times in your life that you have been the one in the holodeck, in the theater of your brain, and people reacted to your communication? You probably thought they were being unreasonable. What may have happened is that they were startled by your communication and became defensive, defensiveness that we may interpret as a personal attack.

Most human thought is subconscious. The conscious part of our thoughts, in fact, represent only the tiniest portion of our computations. Depending on how much in control and able to predict the future we want to be, the more reactive we are going to be to this subconscious processing, and information. If the information being processed is associated with danger, then we will be steering from our present route to avoid danger, creating an experience of chaos.

Now, because we are reacting to this information that we are being fed and this information is associated with immediate and present danger, it doesn't matter what goals or wants we may have and want to fulfill; they will immediately fade out and the sum of our resources will be allocated to address the "immediate and present danger."

Not Every Thought that My Mind Produces Needs to Be Attended to.

As mentioned before, when memories are triggered, we unknowingly and almost immediately take a conscious or subconscious place at the theater in the theater of our minds. So when we are visiting our theater as a response to possible danger and reacting to the fuzzy world over imposed on our movie, we also help trigger the memories of the person we are interacting within that moment, and now there are two people trying to communicate amid the noise of the movies being played in their theater, that for all accounts are real.

However the holodeck and what we are experiencing is happening inside our skull, we are not in an actual place.

Do nothing, you can keep watching the movie and enjoying the popcorn. It is a movie; it's scary, but just a movie.

The physical emotions are due to the movie, do not look for the reasons of your emotions in the present moment. By letting it play, we will experience the moment and the people around us in real time.

Remember that the *Identity* is a form of AI (Artificial Intelligence) that we entrust with our emotional safety and the job of collecting information solidifying and protecting what we believe to be "me".

TWENTY-TWO: What if We don't Have to Matter?

There is no danger in living life as if we don't have to matter at all times. What really matters is being fully engaged in every moment and in everything we do, that's the only thing that actually matters.

Where there is reverence there is fear, but there is not reverence everywhere that there is fear, because fear presumably has a wider extension than reverence.

SOCRATES.

Maybe it's because now it is so clear and simple in my mind what needs to be done to experience reality that all the information leading to this moment seems to look the same. As impatient as I may be, the reality is that this simple concept could not possibly be profoundly understood or experienced without the methodical process of separation from the *Identity*, and the repetition of the consistent buildup of a new system of new neuropaths that will compete with the system of the *Identity*.

If at this point after reading this book you are less reactive in your life, this means that there is a degree of separation and distinction between the *Identity* and who you really are, represented in physiological changes in your brain. There is an awareness of life outside the *Identity*. This has been our goal all along.

The world of the *Identity*, before we create any distinction, is experienced as the whole universe with no concept awareness of anything else. We react and experience threats at every corner and prevailing is all that matters. However, the research being done now validates the conclusion that we are not our brain or our minds. That there is this "self/being" that is able, when activated/accessed, to operate independently from the information the mind is providing. Realizing and being aware on a consistent basis that what my brain is interpreting is not necessarily reality allows me to remain functional and available to more resources.

Being that the mind's main concern when it comes to our emotional experiences is to shield us from pain and fear, it creates a distorted view of the world. It has us reacting to life in a protective way. The brain does not have the ability to distinguish between real physical danger and non-physical emotional danger.

If I am not the voice in my head, the relevance of the stories that my head is bringing is not important. There is nothing we are able to do to quiet the signals of fear that the brain sends when it concludes that there is danger. Fear equals automatic protection and isolation.

In order for us to break free, we have to experience the appropriate emotions, fear, pain, and fear of experiencing pain. These will release the tension. There will be no need to intellectualize and rationalize our way out of pain and fear. Embracing them is all we can do.

Yes, it is difficult to create this separation from our minds since we have co-authored with our brain, our *Identity* but remember that the brain interprets my opinions and my thoughts as if they were the physical me. Any attempt to attack this idea is experienced as a death itself. This is why people say it is "difficult to change," because change implies the "death" of me as I know it.

If the flow of information is not derailed or stopped, this will be the only reality we will ever experience. We see it all over: *I don't believe in men. I will never be successful. I don't believe in women. Life is hard. Life is not fair. I don't trust anyone. People will hurt me.*

Without distinction people with more severe experiences like individuals with severe PTSD or OCD won't be able to dissociate the movie that the brain is featuring from reality; the flow of information will travel fast and far…

Differentiating self from the mind/brain is fundamental to be able to claim a different view of the world, so we can express ourselves in such a way that encourages a fulfilling life.

Studies like "Orbitofrontal cortex neurofeedback", found at:

http://www.nature.com/tp/journal/v3/n4/full/tp2013 24a.html, present us with evidence that when we experience ourselves separate from our brain, we are able to disengage from the information and beliefs that dictated our actions. Help us to understand the impact and the realization that the brain's actions when it comes to interpreting the reality of our emotions is not necessarily the truth, and we are free to explore other possibilities of Being. Being able to realize and disassociate from the responses of the brain, we are able to remain connected to the world outside the thoughts the brain is producing, aware of a reality outside our brains.

What is outside in the world is to be discovered by each of us every minute and every second. I don't know what is in it for you. The only certain thing is that outside we experience belonging, and we are less judgmental and less defensive. The result could be what we call love and everything it represents, patience, caring, etc.

If the *Identity* is a make believe universe within our universe, imagine the *Identity* to be a tent or a crystal dome.

As long as we believe we are the process, the function of the *Identity*, reality will be shuffled to be consistent with those beliefs.

Imagine that the *Identity* is a tent in the middle of a forest but you are missing out on the beauty of it all because you are in this tent. This imagery is for you to become and observer of those processes without intervening or getting involved and to bring the world outside into awareness.

Beliefs are information stored in your brain via neuropaths, and the more information, the more complex the circuitry and the easier for it to react to stimuli. By you becoming an observer, the circuitry will weaken with time and the brain won't have a choice but to create new neuropaths and strengthen some old ones with the information you are exposed to away from the world of the *Identity*. *Identity* will become a faint voice in your life.

There is no danger in living life as if we don't have to matter at all times. With no *Identity* to define you. What really matters is being fully engaged in every moment and in everything we do, that's the only thing that actually matters.

Fear and pain is an intrinsic part of being human. Welcome them in your life, otherwise you will consume all your resources trying to keep them away. There is no mastering fear, and the more we try to keep it at bay the bigger it will grow in our mind.

Acknowledge that you are "in" to bring the awareness that there is "out" so you can start discovering the forest around you.

If everything fails, there is always this:

https://www.youtube.com/watch?v=Ow0lr63y4Mw